Test Better, Teach Better

The Instructional Role of Assessment

W. James Popham

Test
Better,
Teach
Better

The Instructional Role of Assessment

Association for Supervision and Curriculum Development • Alexandria, Virginia USA

Association for Supervision and Curriculum Development
1703 N. Beauregard St. • Alexandria, VA 22311-1714 USA
Telephone: 800-933-2723 or 703-578-9600 • Fax: 703-575-5400
Web site: http://www.ascd.org • E-mail: member@ascd.org
Author guidelines: www.ascd.org/write

Gene R. Carter, *Executive Director;* Nancy Modrak, *Director of Publishing;* Julie Houtz, *Director of Book Editing & Production;* Katie Martin, *Project Manager;* Georgia McDonald, *Senior Graphic Designer;* Valerie Sprague and Keith Demmons, *Desktop Publishers.*

All Web links in this book are correct as of the publication date below but may have become inactive or otherwise modified since that time. If you notice a deactivated or changed link, please e-mail books@ascd.org with the words "Link Update" in the subject line. In your message, please specify the Web link, the book title, and the page number on which the link appears.

Printed in the United States of America.

s8/03

ISBN-13: 978-0-87120-667-1   ISBN-10: 0-87120-667-6

ASCD product no.: 102088

Also available as an e-book through ebrary, netLibrary, and many online booksellers (see Books in Print for the ISBNs).

Library of Congress Cataloging-in-Publication Data

Popham, W. James.
  Test better, teach better : the instructional role of assessment / W. James Popham.
      p. cm.
Includes bibliographical references and index.
  ISBN 0-87120-667-6 (alk. paper)
  1. Educational tests and measurements. 2. Examinations. 3. Effective teaching. I. Title.

  LB3051.P61433 2003
  371.26′2—dc21
                              2003011511

12 11 10 09 08 07   12 11 10 9 8 7 6 5 4

Preface

IF YOU COULD MAGICALLY AND SURREPTITIOUSLY SLIP INTO THE BACK OF ANY American classroom these days, odds are you'd find the students taking a test. At least that's the way it must seem to most of our nation's teachers. More and more frequently, teachers find themselves obliged to give their students state-mandated or district-mandated tests that they work in amongst their own classroom testing practices. "Recess" used to mean a time when students were let out to play. Now, at least to many teachers, it's a blessed week in which teachers are not required to administer some sort of externally imposed test.

Accountability Pressures and a New Federal Law

The chief reason for what seems to be an explosion of educational testing is that U.S. educational policymakers, bent on making the nation's educators more accountable, want hard evidence regarding how well public schools are performing. These policymakers, and most of our citizens as well, believe that student test performance should be the ultimate yardstick by which we measure a school's effectiveness. Naturally, then, teachers are under pressure to raise their students' test scores. You know the logic: High test scores signify good schooling and low test scores signify bad schooling.

The already thriving national obsession with educational testing intensified in early 2002, when President George W. Bush signed the

No Child Left Behind (NCLB) Act, an enormously significant piece of federal legislation laced with loads of assessment-and-accountability provisions. The most widely publicized of these, set to take effect in the 2005–2006 school year, is a requirement for every state to conduct achievement testing in reading and mathematics: once a year for all students in grades 3–8 and at least once again in high school, prior to graduation. In addition, NCLB also requires every state to carry out science assessments in several grade ranges, beginning in the 2007–2008 school year. Given the availability of the data these tests will generate, it's certain that NCLB-sired test results will play a prominent role in state-level accountability systems that associate student scores with school and teacher quality.

From a teacher's perspective, however, it is difficult to figure out why more mandated testing will lead to a higher quality of instruction—especially as current accountability-spawned educational tests results have little utility *in the classroom.* In fact, many teachers find that the instructional benefits provided by today's required educational tests are almost nonexistent. Too rarely do teachers find that a student's performance on these tests helps diagnose that student's strengths and weaknesses. Too rarely do teachers find that a student's test performance gives them a better idea of what it is they need to do instructionally to help that student achieve better results. The result of this high pressure with little educational benefit is that more and more teachers associate *testing* with something negative—something to be dreaded or "dealt with" rather something to be embraced as illuminating, helpful, and even essential to better learning. And yet, if properly conceived, educational testing *is* illuminating, helpful, and even essential to better learning. In the pages that follow, I'll try to show you why.

The Intended Medicine

Too much testing has become a sort of sickness in some schools. But tests—the right kinds of tests—*can* give teachers really powerful insights about how best to teach their students. And teaching students, of course, is the reason most folks chose to become teachers in the first place. Yet, the distressing reality is that teachers who do not possess at least rudimentary knowledge about *testing* are less likely to do a solid job of *teaching*. And that's what this book is about: the kind of testing that improves one's teaching.

I wrote this book for three types of readers:

• Experienced teachers who were not required to complete coursework in educational testing during their preservice teacher-education days. There are many such teachers.

• Experienced teachers who may have taken a course in educational measurement but found the course's theoretical orientation unrelated to the real-world travails of the classroom. There are lots of these teachers as well.

• Students in teacher-education programs who, perhaps in connection with a course in instructional methods or educational psychology, have been asked by their instructor to take a serious look at educational testing. I *hope* there are many such teacher-education students!

All right, now that I've told you for whom I wrote the book, let me tell you why I wrote it and what you'll find here. I wrote this book to inform educators, and those preparing to be educators, about some basic things they need to know regarding educational testing. More specifically, I want to help teachers master a set of measurement-related skills and knowledge they'll need if they are going to teach their students effectively.

Instructionally Focused Testing: Two Species

There are really two kinds of educational tests that may (or may not) help teachers do a better instructional job. The first is a teacher's *classroom tests*, typically designed by the teacher to measure student mastery of specific unit content. The second is *externally imposed tests,* those tests required by state or district authorities and designed by professional test developers to measure student mastery of the sets of objectives experts have deemed essential.

Because teachers obviously have far more influence over tests they create for their own students, I've devoted the majority of this book to the innards of teacher-made classroom tests and the measurement concepts that have a direct bearing on classroom test construction and use. But, given the test-obsessed reality most teachers are living in, I have also addressed several issues related to external testing. Teachers must become more familiar with the uses and misuses of externally imposed tests so that they can recognize when an unsound test is being forced on their students, protest persuasively against such testing, and, over time, influence these tests' revision. Thus, as you read through this book, you'll see that some content pertains exclusively to classroom tests, some content pertains only to external tests, and some content pertains to both.

Two Books About Testing: Comparing and Contrasting

Not so long ago, I wrote a book called *The Truth About Testing,* also published by the Association for Supervision and Curriculum Development (ASCD). Because both books deal with educational testing, it's possible that some confusion could arise about the two books' treatment of the topic. I thought a few sentences dealing directly with this matter might be helpful.

The Truth About Testing is subtitled *An Educator's Call to Action.* I wrote it to inform educators of several assessment-induced problems that I believe are eroding the quality of schooling in the United States. I tried to explain those test-related problems, and then I laid out a series of actions educators could take to deal with the situation. In short, *The Truth About Testing* is an experience-based entreaty to my educational colleagues (influential educational leaders especially) to *do something* to fix the problems resulting from the use of the wrong kinds of tests in our schools. In contrast, the book you're reading now represents an attempt to familiarize teachers with the kinds of assessment practicalities they need so that they can get the most out of their own classroom tests and ensure, insofar as possible, that any externally imposed assessments their students take are educationally defensible.

Do the two books overlap? Yes, at certain points they do, because there are some assessment-related concepts that are so significant that they need to be understood by *every educator*. For example, in both books, I've tried hard to get readers to realize why it is that traditionally constructed standardized achievement tests are having such an adverse affect on U.S. education. I believe that both current and future teachers need to understand the reasons underlying this problem. However, *The Truth About Testing* gave little if any attention to the creation and use of the kinds of classroom tests that I describe in this book. That's because classroom teachers really do need to know how to provide care and feeding for varied sorts of test items. The current book, then, is not a "call to action," but a guide to better test use.

A Plunge into the Pool of Practical Assessment

With the *why-I-wrote-this* covered, let's turn to content. I promise that everything about testing that you will read in this book will have a direct bearing on classroom-based instructional decision making. In fact, to keep me honest, and to help you tie a mental ribbon around each chapter, I've concluded each of the book's 11 chapters with a set of "Instructionally Focused Testing Tips," a few concise points clarifying the most salient implications for classroom teachers.

I'd like to make one last point before you proceed to the rest of the book. This is a short book, a book deliberately written for busy people. Instead of providing a comprehensive treatment of these topics, I've synthesized the important ideas that focus on *what matters most* to teachers faced with instructional decisions. As you read through my nuts-and-bolts coverage, you are almost certain to encounter some topics about which you'd like to learn more. Obligingly, at the end of each chapter, I've provided a set of recommended resources to guide more detailed excursions into the topics treated briefly here.

You can think of this book as a crash course in instructionally focused testing. If you are an experienced teacher, you'll be able to roll through the entire thing in an evening or two. If you are a student in a teacher-education program, then read what your professor says to read! But regardless of your reading rate, I can assure you that mastery of the concepts I present here will help you teach better. And if you teach better, then your students will learn better.

Faced with such persuasive logic, how can you wait any longer to get started?

The Links Between Testing and Teaching

YOU'D PROBABLY FIND IT DIFFICULT TO LOCATE ANYONE, TEACHER OR NON-teacher, who doesn't recognize that there's *some* sort of a relationship between teaching and testing. Just about everyone realizes that if a teacher does a great instructional job, that teacher's students will usually perform better on tests. It's the other side of the equation that's less often understood, namely, that *how* a teacher tests—the way a teacher designs tests and applies test data—can profoundly affect *how well* that teacher teaches.

The connection between one's teaching and one's testing is a critical one that, if properly understood, can lead to a substantial increase in instructional effectiveness. I want you not only to accept the idea that testing can help teaching, but also *to act* on that idea. I want you to pick up tangible instructional payoffs from linking your tests to your teaching. You'll teach better, and your students will learn more. You'll be a better teacher, and I'll be a happy author. Let's get started.

What's in a Name?

I need to define some terms as we get under way. First, what is a *test* or, more specifically, what is an *educational test?* Simply put, an educational test is a formal attempt to determine a student's status with respect to specific variables, such as the student's knowledge, skills, and attitudes. The adjective "formal" in the previous sentence is important, because it distinguishes a test from the many casual judgments that teachers routinely make about their students. For example, during my first year of teaching (in a small eastern Oregon high school), I had a student named Mary Ruth Green. I could almost always tell (or so I thought) how well Mary Ruth had mastered the previous night's English homework assignment. When it came time to discuss the homework topic, if Mary Ruth was animated and eager to contribute, I concluded that she knew the assigned stuff. If she sat silently and avoided eye contact with me, however, I guessed that she and the previous night's homework topic were unacquainted.

I made all sorts of on-the-spot judgments about what Mary Ruth and my other students knew, but those judgments were informal ones and often based on pretty skimpy observational data. In contrast, a test entails a systematic effort to get a fix on a student's status with respect to such things as the student's ability to perform an intellectual skill—to compose a job-application letter, for instance, or to carry out an hypothesis-testing experiment in a chemistry class.

For many people, the word *test* conjures up images of traditional, paper-and-pencil forms (multiple-choice exams or True-False quizzes). Perhaps this explains why a growing number of educators prefer to use the term *assessment,* which seems to embrace both traditional forms of testing and comparatively recent ones like looking for evidence of learning by examining student-generated work portfolios or group reports of experimental projects. Still, as long as you don't restrict yourself to only traditional testing approaches, the terms *test* and *assessment* are really interchangeable. And while we're swimming in this particular synonym pool, let me toss in two more: the slightly technical-sounding *measurement* and the serious-sounding *examination* (or *exam*). Each of these four terms describes a formal attempt to determine a student's status with respect to an educationally relevant variable. In this book, you'll find that I use all four interchangeably, not for any subtle reasons, but just because I get tired of using the same word all the time.

Why We Test

Human beings are tough to figure out. Ask any psychiatrist. Ask yourself. And young human beings in grades K–12 are no exception. To illustrate, if a teacher wants to determine what Ted's ability to read is, the teacher won't find that information tattooed on Ted's arm. Ted's reading ability is *covert*. The teacher must figure out how to uncover that hidden ability. So the teacher whips up a 15-item reading test calling for Ted to read several short passages and then answer a series of questions getting at (1) the central messages in the passages and (2) certain key details in those passages. Ted takes the test and does a great job, answering each of the 15 items correctly. The teacher then makes an *inference* about Ted's covert reading ability based on Ted's overt performance on the 15-item test.

If you think about it, just about every worthwhile thing that educators try to promote is unseeable. Consider spelling ability as another example. A child's spelling ability cannot be seen, only inferred. What goes through the teacher's head is something like this:

> Martha did well on this month's spelling test. She wrote out "from scratch" the correct spellings for 18 of 20 words I read out loud. It is reasonable for me to infer, then, that Martha possesses a really high level of spelling ability—a level of ability that would display itself in a fairly similar fashion if Martha were asked to take other, similar 20-item spelling tests.

Remember, what the teacher sees when Martha spells the word "awry" properly is only Martha's spelling of "awry" and *not* Martha's spelling ability. The teacher needs to *infer* the level of Martha's spelling skill by seeing how well Martha does on her spelling tests. The more spelling tests that Martha takes, the more confidence the teacher can have in any inferences about Martha's spelling skill. An inference about a student can be based on a single test; a more accurate inference will be made if multiple tests are employed.

Likewise, a child's ability to perform basic arithmetic skills is unseeable; it's something we infer from the child's performance on an exam (or, preferably, more than one exam) dealing with adding, subtracting, multiplying, and dividing. Children's confidence in being able to present an oral report to their classmates is certainly unseeable, but again, we can infer it from students' responses to an assessment instrument constructed specifically to measure such things. (You'll learn more about that sort of noncognitive assessment in Chapter 8.)

So educational measurement is, at bottom, *an inference-making enterprise* in which we formally collect overt, test-based evidence from students to arrive at what we hope are accurate inferences about students' status with respect to covert, educationally important variables: reading ability, knowledge of history, ability to solve simultaneous equations, interest in social studies, and so on. The process is represented in Figure 1.1.

1.1　EDUCATIONAL TESTING AS AN INFERENCE-MAKING PROCESS

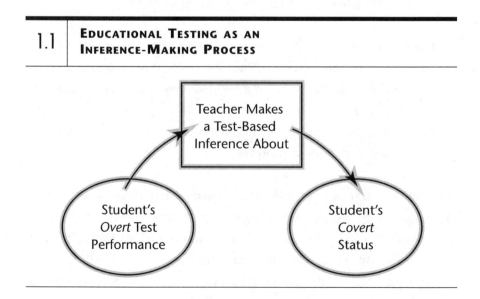

Teacher Makes a Test-Based Inference About

Student's *Overt* Test Performance

Student's *Covert* Status

Yes, as my experience with Mary Ruth and her homework showed, it is certainly possible for a teacher to make an inference about students based on informal, nontest evidence. Suppose your student Alvin gives you a note in which he had misspelled several words. Based on this evidence, you might infer that Alvin's spelling ability isn't all that wonderful. However, a *formal* assessment of Alvin's spelling skill, one based on a larger and more age-appropriate set of words, would increase the likelihood of your making an accurate inference about Alvin's spelling ability.

The accuracy of these inferences is critical, because a teacher's understanding of students' knowledge, abilities, and attitudes should form the basis for the teacher's instructional decisions. And, of course, the more accurate the test-based inferences a teacher makes, the more defensible will be the teacher's instructional decisions based on those inferences.

What Sorts of Teaching Decisions Can Tests Help?

I've been touting the tight relationship that should be present between testing and teaching. It's time to get more specific. There are four types of teaching decisions that should rest squarely on what a teacher finds out either from the structure of the educational tests themselves or from the way students perform on educational tests.

Decisions about the nature and purpose of the curriculum. Essentially, the teacher seeks answers to questions like these: "What am I really trying to teach? What do my students need to know and be able to do? How can I translate the big curricular goals set for my students into specific, teachable components?"

Decisions about students' prior knowledge. Questions include, "What do my students already know about the topic I'm planning to teach? Are there any gaps that I need to address before we can tackle this material? Based on what my students know and can do, how can I tailor my instruction to provide the proper balance of remediation and challenge?"

Decisions about how long to teach something. Questions include, "How long do I think it will take my students to master this content? What kind of progress are they making? Are we on the right track? Should I continue teaching on my planned schedule, or are we ready to move on?"

Decisions about the effectiveness of instruction. Questions include, "Did my students learn? Was the instructional approach I took a good one? What specific activities were the most advantageous? Where do I need to make alterations?"

Now, let's take a closer look at how tests—both their design and the results of their application—can help teachers make these kinds of decisions with confidence.

Using Tests to Clarify the Curriculum

Typically, educators think of a curriculum as the set of intended outcomes that we want students to achieve. During the bulk of my teaching career, most teachers have used the phrase *educational objectives* to describe their curricular intentions. These days, of course, we find that most curricula are described as sets of *content standards*— that is, the knowledge and skills students are supposed to master as a consequence of instruction. Sometimes we see the term *benchmarks* used to describe the more specific skills and knowledge often subsumed beneath fairly broad content standards. The descriptors may change, but the mission of a curriculum remains constant: Its essential purpose is to lay out the stuff we want kids to learn.

Regardless of whether we call them content standards, goals, or objectives, the curricular intentions handed down by states and districts are often less clear than teachers need them to be for purposes of day-to-day instructional planning. For example, a group of elementary teachers might find themselves responsible for promoting this district-approved social studies content standard: "Students will comprehend the formal and informal nature of the interrelationships among the executive, legislative, and judicial branches of U.S. government."

Let's imagine you're one of the 5th grade teachers who is supposed to help students master this content standard. How would you go about planning your instruction? Personally, I think there's way too much fuzz on this curricular peach. Different teachers could easily read this social studies content standard and come up with quite divergent ideas of what it signifies. For example, one teacher might conclude that this content standard focuses exclusively on the formal and informal "checks and balances" when one governmental branch interacts with the other two. Another teacher might think that this content standard emphasizes the distinction between "formal" and "informal" interrelationships among the three governmental branches.

Now suppose that your 5th graders will be taking an important "standards-based" social studies achievement test at the end of the school year. If the people who built that test interpret this social studies content standard in one way, and you interpret it in another way—and *teach toward your interpretation*—it's almost certain that your students won't do as well on the achievement test as you, your principal, or your students' parents would like.

Clearly, if the curricular aims that a teacher must address are open to multiple interpretations, then off-the-mark instruction is likely to occur, bringing with it lower test performances. But if a curricular goal is accompanied by a set of illustrative test items indicating the ways that the goal will be measured, then teachers can analyze those items and form a far more accurate idea of the outcome that the state or district is actually seeking. Because the sample test items exemplify what the curricular intention really represents, teachers can plan and provide their students with better, more curricularly relevant instruction.

To illustrate, suppose you knew that mastery of the fairly fuzzy 5th grade social studies goal about the three branches of the U.S. government would be assessed by items similar to the following:

SAMPLE ITEM 1

Which of the following three branches of U.S. government, if any, is primarily responsible for the final enactment of treaties with foreign nations?

    a. Legislative   c. Judicial

    b. Executive   d. No single branch is responsible.

SAMPLE ITEM 2

Which, if any, of the following statements about governmental stability is true? (Mark each statement as True or False.)

a. The enactment of term-limiting legislation at the local level has made the U.S. federal legislative branch of government more stable.

b. The availability of the impeachment process tends to decrease the stability of the executive branch of U.S. government.

c. Historically, the judicial branch of U.S. federal government has been the most stable.

SAMPLE ITEM 3

Our founding fathers charted a meaningful series of governmental checks and balances. Focus on the area of **taxation,** then select two of the three branches and briefly describe the *formal* way(s) in which one branch can check the other. Answer in the space provided below.

_____

_____

_____

Having read these sample items, wouldn't you have a much better idea of what to teach your students in order for them to come to *"comprehend the formal and informal nature of the interrelationships among the executive, legislative, and judicial branches of U.S. government*"? Sample Item 1 makes it clear that students will need to learn the primary responsibilities of each governmental branch. Sample Item 2 suggests that students must learn *why* important factors such as governmental stability are present for each branch. And Sample Item 3 indicates that, as the content standard said, students will need to understand the "formal and informal nature of the relationships" among the governmental branches. For this item, as you can see, the focus is on *formal*. In another item, you can reasonably assume, the focus might be on *informal*. Moreover, Sample Item 3 tips you off that students may need to display this understanding by constructing their own responses, rather than merely selecting a response from a set of options.

I believe that elementary teachers who consider these three illustrative items along with the original statement of the content standard are going to have a far more lucid idea of what the content standard actually means. Consequently, they'll be able to deliver instruction that is more on-target and more effective.

The payoffs from test-triggered clarity about curriculum goals can apply with equal force to a teacher's own, personally chosen curricular aspirations. If teachers are pursuing curricular aims of their own choosing, but those aims are less clear (in a teacher's mind) than is desirable for instructional planning purposes, then teachers are likely to come up with less relevant instruction. To illustrate, when I was a first-year teacher, I wanted the students in my two English classes "to be better writers." But even though that very general goal was in my mind as the school year got under way, I really had no idea of what it meant for my students to be "better writers." As the months went by, I occasionally had my students write a practice essay. However, for their final exam, I had them answer multiple-choice items about the mechanics of writing. Shame on me!

The task of creating a few sample assessment items can bring the desired outcomes into focus. In short, test-exemplified curricular goals will almost always be better promoted instructionally than will unexemplified curricular goals. Because of the significance of tests in helping teachers clarify their instructional targets, I'm going to dig into this topic a bit more deeply in Chapter 2. Stay tuned.

Using Tests to Determine Students' Entry Status

In most instructional settings, teachers inherit a new crop of students each year, and more often than not, these teachers really don't know what sorts of capabilities the new students bring with them. Likewise, teachers looking ahead in their planning books to new topics or skills (weather systems, Homer's epics, multiplying fractions, group discussion skills, ability to work independently) frequently find they have only the roughest idea, usually based on the previous grade level's content standards, of their students' existing familiarity or interest in the upcoming topics or of their students' expertise in the upcoming skill areas. Knowing where students stand in relation to future content, both as a group and as individuals, is one of a teacher's most valuable tools in planning appropriate and engaging instruction. Therefore, it's an eminently sensible thing for teachers to get a fix on their students' entry status by pre-assessing them, usually using teacher-created tests to find out what sorts of skills, knowledge, or attitudes these students have. The more diagnostic a pretest is, the more illuminating it will be to the teacher.

You can use pretests to isolate the things your new students already know as well as the things you will need to teach them. If you are a middle school English teacher aspiring to have your 8th graders write gripping narrative essays, and you're certain that these 8th graders haven't seriously studied narrative essays during their earlier years in school, you could use a pre-assessment to help you determine whether your students possess important *enabling* subskills. Can they, for example, write sentences and paragraphs largely free of mechanical errors in spelling, punctuation, and word usage? If their pre-assessment results show that they already possess these enabling subskills, there's no need to *re-teach* such subskills. If the pre-assessment results show that your students' mastery of the mechanics of writing is modest, then you'll need to devote appropriate time to promoting such subskills before you move on.

This example brings up an important point. If you're using a classroom pretest chiefly to get a picture of what your students already can do regarding a particular content standard, you should always try to employ a pretest that covers the standard's key enabling subskills or bodies of knowledge. For instance, when I taught a speech class in high school, I always had my students deliver a two- to three-minute extemporaneous speech early in the term. I was looking particularly for the fundamentals—posture, eye contact, organization of content, introductions, conclusions, and avoidance time-fillers such as "uh" and "you know"—those things I knew students needed to master before they could work on refining their abilities as first-class public speakers. Those pretests helped me decide where I wanted to aim my early instruction, and it was always at the most serious weaknesses the students displayed during their "mini-orations."

Using Tests to Determine How Long to Teach Something

One of the classes I taught in my early years on the "grown-up" side of the desk was 10th grade geography. Thanks to a blessed red geography textbook and my ability to read more rapidly than my 10th graders, I survived the experience (barely). I remember that one of my units was three-week focus on map projections and map skills, during which we explored the use of such map-types as Mercator and homolographic projections. Each year that I taught 10th grade geography, my three-week unit on maps was always precisely three weeks in length. I never altered the duration of the unit because, after all, I had originally estimated that it would take 15 days of teaching to stuff the designated content into my students' heads. Yes, I was instructionally naïve. Beginning teachers often are.

What I should have done instead was use some sort of "dipstick" assessment of students' map skills throughout that three-week period to give me a better idea of how long I really needed to keep teaching map skills to my 10th graders. I always gave my students a 30-item map skills exam at the end of the 3 weeks; I could easily have taken that exam and split it up into 15 microquizzes of 1 or 2 items each, and then randomly administered each of those microquizzes to different students at the end of, say, 2 weeks. Students would have needed only two or three minutes to complete their microquizzes.

This approach is a form of what's called *item sampling*, a manner of testing in which different students are asked to complete different subsamples of items from a test. It works quite well if a teacher is trying to get a fix on the status of an entire class. (Clearly, item sampling wouldn't permit sensible inferences about individual students because different students would be completing different microquizzes.) By reviewing the results of my item-sampled, *en route* assessment, I could have determined whether, at the end of only two weeks, my students had already learned enough from their meanderings through Mapland. Looking back, I suspect, we continued to mess with Mercators and homolographics well beyond what was necessary.

You can do something similar with your own students to help you decide how long to continue teaching toward a particular content standard. By using an occasional *en route* test (either item sampling or by giving the same, possibly shortened, test to all of your students), you can tell whether you need to keep banging away on a topic or can put your drumsticks away.

This kind of instructionally illuminating testing, sometimes referred to as *formative assessment,* is a particularly valuable tool today, when there's so much to fit into each school year. The time saved in an easily mastered unit can be time applied to other material that students have unexpected difficulty with. Flexible, *en route* test-guided instructional scheduling can allow your students to move on to fascinating application activities or delve more deeply into other content.

Using Tests to Determine the Effectiveness of Instruction

The issue of how well a teacher has taught is becoming more and more critical as the educational accountability movement places teachers under ever-intensifying scrutiny. The folks who are demanding evidence that teachers are doing a solid instructional job are looking for hard evidence that proves instructional effectiveness.

This is such a serious and complicated assessment-related issue that I've devoted three chapters in this book to it. Chapter 9 explores how *not* to evaluate a teacher's effectiveness; Chapters 10 and 11 tell how to go about it properly. But, because finding out how effective your own instruction is should be important to you, I need to address some important assessment-related topics first.

These days, many teachers' instructional competence is being determined on the basis of a single achievement test administered to students each spring. For instance, a 4th grade teacher's students complete a state-approved standardized achievement test in May, and then the test results of this year's 4th graders are compared with the test results of last year's 4th graders. If this year's scores are better than last year's scores, the 4th grade teacher is thought to be doing a good instructional job . . . and vice versa.

But this sort of teacher-appraisal model flunks on several counts. For one thing, it relies on the wrong kind of measurement tool, as you'll learn when you get to Chapter 9. And there's another, more obvious shortcoming in these year-to-year comparison models. The problem is that each year's testing takes place with *a different group of students,* and the results depend on the collection of kids being compared. If your students last year were an atypical collection of gifted girls and boys and this year's crop is a more typical mix, then you can expect your year-to-year results to show a decline, regardless of your abilities as an instructor.

The simple little model of pre-assessment and postassessment comparison displayed in Figure 1.2 is the most fundamental way teachers can judge their own teaching skill. A pretest gets a fix on students' status before instruction (at the start of school year, say) and a post-test measures the same students' status again, once instruction is complete (at the end of the school year).

1.2   A COMMON MODEL FOR DETERMINING INSTRUMENTAL IMPACT

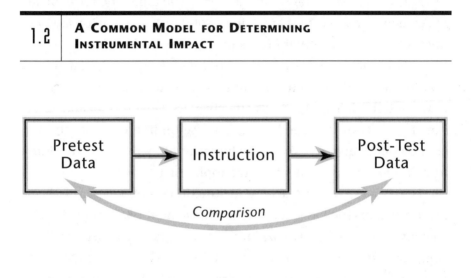

As you can see from the figure, the heart of this evaluative model is students' test performance. Although a *teacher's* overall performance should be determined using a variety of evaluative considerations, not just students' test data, one overridingly important factor should be how well the teacher's students have learned what they were supposed to learn. A pretest/post-test evaluative approach (using some refinements that you'll read about in Chapter 11) can contribute meaningfully to how teachers determine their own instructional impact.

Okay, we've considered four ways in which testing—the tests themselves and the student results they produce—can help a teacher make better instructional decisions. The rest of this book will provide you with sufficient information about these and other ways of using assessment in your own classes to make your instructional decisions more defensible.

INSTRUCTIONALLY FOCUSED TESTING TIPS

- Recognize that students' overt responses to educational tests allow teachers to make inferences about students' covert status.
- Use tests to exemplify—and, thus, clarify—fuzzy statements of curricular aims.
- Pre-assess any new group of students to identify those students' entry status. Also pre-assess students when they'll be encountering new skills and knowledge to be learned.
- Use test results to determine how much instruction on a given topic your students need.
- Include the data generated by educational tests in evaluations of your own instructional effectiveness.

Recommended Resources

Falk, B. (2000). *The heart of the matter: Using standards and assessment to learn.* Westport, CT: Heinemann.

Popham, W. J. (Program Consultant). (1996). *Improving instruction through classroom assessment* [Videotape]. Los Angeles: IOX Assessment Associates.

Popham, W. J. (2001). *The truth about testing: An educator's call to action*: Alexandria, VA: Association for Supervision and Curriculum Development.

Popham, W. J. (Program Consultant). (2002). *Educational tests: Misunderstood measuring sticks* [Videotape]. Los Angeles: IOX Assessment Associates.

Ramirez, A. (1999, November). Assessment-driven reform: The emperor still has no clothes. *Phi Delta Kappan, 81*(3), 204–208.

Shepard, L. A. (2000, October). The role of assessment in a learning culture. *Educational Researcher, 29*(7), 4–14.

Sirotnik, K. A., & Kimball, K. (1999, November). Standards for standards-based accountability systems. *Phi Delta Kappan, 81*(3), 209–214.

Stiggins, R. J. (Program Consultant). (1996). *Creating sound classroom assessments* [Videotape]. Portland, OR: Assessment Training Institute.

Stiggins, R. J. (2001). *Student-involved classroom assessment* (4th ed.). Upper Saddle River, NJ: Prentice Hall.

Wiggins, G., Stiggins, R. J., Moses, M., & LeMahieu, P. (Program Consultants). (1991). *Redesigning assessment: Introduction* [Videotape]. Alexandria, VA: Association for Supervision and Curriculum Development.

How Tests Can Clarify the Curriculum

2

TEACHERS WHO TRULY UNDERSTAND WHAT THEY WANT THEIR STUDENTS TO accomplish will almost surely be more instructionally successful than teachers whose understanding of hoped-for student accomplishments are murky. In this chapter, I'll elaborate on how educational tests can help teachers get a clearer idea of the direction in which their instruction ought to be headed.

When I talk about *curriculum* and *instruction*, I use both terms in a fairly traditional fashion. By "curriculum," I mean the outcomes that educators hope to achieve with their students. The three most common kinds of outcomes sought are students' acquisition of *cognitive skills* (such as being able to multiply pairs of triple-digit numbers); their acquisition of bodies of *knowledge* (such as understanding chlorophyll's role in photosynthesis); and their *affect* (such as particular attitudes, interests, or values). When I use the word "instruction," I am thinking of the activities that educators carry out in order to help their students attain those intended outcomes. As Figure 2.1 illustrates, curriculum and instruction can be understood as educational *ends* and educational *means*.

Although teachers often make their own decisions about which educational ends they want their students to achieve, in most

| 2.1 | THE RELATIONSHIP BETWEEN CURRICULUM AND INSTRUCTION |

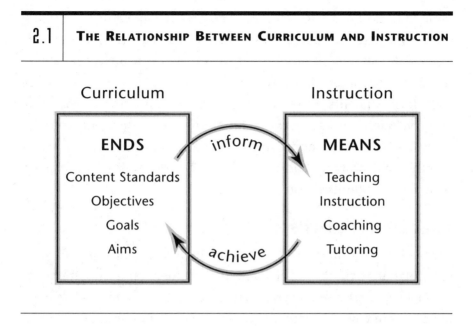

instances these days, higher authorities (district or state officials) stipulate what those ends ought to be. Still, it's almost always up to teachers to devise the instructional activities (the means) they believe will achieve those particular ends. For example, a high school English teacher trying to get students to become skilled writers of persuasive essays (a state-approved curricular outcome) might plan a four-week unit giving students plenty of guided and independent practice composing such essays. Other instructional tactics might include providing solid models of well-written persuasive essays for students to review, having students critique each other's draft essays, and arranging for a motivational visit from an editorial writer at the local newspaper. Together, all these activities constitute the teacher's instruction and, thus, represent the teacher's best judgment about the means that are necessary to accomplish a particular curricular end.

As indicated earlier, a teacher who is clear about what the curricular ends are will almost always come up with more successful instructional means than will a teacher who has only a muddle-minded notion of what a curricular end really represents. And that's precisely where educational assessments can help. Tests can enable teachers to get a more meaningful fix on what it really is that a curricular aim (a content standard, goal, objective, or intended outcome) seeks from students. Some teachers may think it odd that they can glean valuable information not just from test results, but from an analysis of test design and from designing tests themselves. But that's exactly what properly constructed tests can do, well in advance of their actual administration.

Three Instructional Payoffs

What, then, are the real-world instructional dividends of clarifying curricular aims via tests? There are three of them, and they are huge.

More accurate task analyses. When you have a better understanding of where your final destination is, you can more sensibly identify any necessary knowledge or skills that students will either need to possess already or that you must teach them along the way. The more accurately you can single out any key enabling subskills or enabling knowledge that your students must possess, the greater the odds that you will address those enabling subskills or knowledge in your instruction.

Clearer explanations. Have you ever tried to explain something to someone when you yourself were less than 100 percent clear about what you were yammering about? I have, and I always knew deep down that my explanations were more than a mite muddy. Test-induced clarity about what a given content standard really means will help you to supply your students with more coherent, more accurate explanations.

More appropriate practice activities. Practice exercises, both guided practice and independent practice, are terrifically important, especially if you are seeking high-level curricular outcomes. In my own teaching experience, whenever my instruction turned out poorly, it was almost always because I had failed to give my students sufficient practice activities, that is, sufficient *time-on-task* exercises. Both experience and empirical research indicate that time-on-task exercises, accompanied by immediate feedback for students, are a key ingredient in stellar instruction. If practice activities miss the mark because of a teacher's misunderstanding about what an educational objective truly represents, then students won't learn as well. If you use tests to exemplify educational objectives, you'll understand those objectives better and be able to incorporate on-the-mark practice activities into your lessons.

To sum up, teachers who clarify their curricular aims by using tests to illustrate what those aims really signify will be able to devise more effective instructional means to promote students' mastery of test-clarified curricular ends. In concert, these three instructional advantages—*improved task analyses, clearer explanations,* and *more on-target practice activities*—are genuinely potent.

How Assessments Can Clarify Curricular Aims

Recall that educational tests are employed to secure *overt* (visible) evidence from students so that teachers can make an inference about the *covert* (unseen) status of their students. Collecting data to support wise inferences is the essence of educational measurement.

As a school-world reality, however, many of the curricular aims that teachers encounter come in the forms of content standards stated so generally that it's tough to get an accurate sense of what the curricular aim really signifies. That's certainly true for many of today's content standards. If you study any set of state-approved or district-approved content standards, you'll almost always find a few that will force you to wonder aloud about the nature of the curricular aim that's being sought. I still remember my all-time favorite opaque curricular aim, a state-approved language arts objective: "Students will learn to relish literature." I'm sure the educators who devised this curricular aim had some sort of idea about what they wanted students to be able to do at the completion of instruction, but as written, I daresay most teachers would be more than a little unclear about what this chopped-pickle objective really represents. (Incidentally, I have yet to encounter an objective calling for students "to mayonnaise mathematics." But there's still time!)

To cope with overly general curricular aims, educators can take a lesson from the tactics of experimental psychologists who, because they frequently deal with covert and elusive human attributes (things like a person's "motivation," "anxiety," or "happiness") have come up with a strategy for clarifying covert variables. The psychologist first describes an overt behavior, such as a person's tendency to persevere unproductively when attempting to solve a problem or perform a task. Then the psychologist chooses an overt operation to represent these covert "perseveration tendencies." This might be the number of times a person continues to press a lever after a lever-press fails to yield the silver dollars previously awarded by each and every lever-press. The psychologist signifies that the number of unrewarded lever-presses a person makes represents that individual's perseveration tendencies. The more unrewarded lever-presses the person makes, the stronger that person's tendency to perseverate.

What the experimental psychologist does is *operationalize* the meaning of a covert variable by setting up an operation to yield a quantifiable result that, in effect, serves as a proxy for the variable being studied. Educators do much the same thing when they use a student's performance on a 25-item spelling test (an overt operation) to represent a student's spelling ability (a covert variable).

Because most curricular aims are stated quite generally, there are different ways a teacher might operationalize any given aim. To illustrate, let's consider a common language arts goal related to a student's reading comprehension. Suppose you were trying to measure your students' ability to identify main ideas in paragraphs. You might operationalize this ill-defined skill by asking your students to read a series of paragraphs (each with a reasonably discernible main idea) and then asking them to do one or more of the following things:

• Write an accurate statement of any paragraph's main idea.

• Select from four-option, multiple-choice items the best statement of a given paragraph's main idea.

• Orally, provide a reasonable paraphrase of any paragraph's main idea.

Notice that each of these ways of operationalizing a student's ability to discern a paragraph's main idea revolves around the student's chief cognitive task in main-idea detection: ferreting out the paragraph's central message, whether implied or explicit. What you must remember as you consider how this or any other curricular aim has been operationalized by a test is that the specific testing approach being used is often only one way of operationalizing the covert knowledge, skills, or affect staked out in the form of a curricular aim. Nevertheless, each of these operationalizations is slightly different and, as a consequence, might lead you toward somewhat different sorts of instructional plans.

Dissimilar Assessments, Dissimilar Instruction

To illustrate how it is that different ways of assessing students' curricular mastery will often lead to different instructional approaches, suppose you are a 4th grade teacher charged with promoting your students' mastery of a state-stipulated language arts goal in reading described only as "increasing students' ability to comprehend the main ideas in paragraphs."

As we just saw, there are numerous ways that this fairly loose curricular aim might be operationalized. Let's say you discover that a newly developed statewide achievement test for 4th graders attempts to measure this skill exclusively by designating particular paragraphs in somewhat lengthy "authentic" passages, and then requiring students to select from four multiple-choice options the best statement of a designated paragraph's main idea. Based on this operationalization, what kind of instruction would help students achieve this objective?

First, you'd definitely want your lessons to incorporate plenty of practice time dealing with the intellectual skills students need to master this sort of multiple-choice test item. You would need to help your students make the kinds of discriminations they would need to make between "best" and "less than best" options in a multiple-choice test item. You might have your students read a paragraph and then lead an exploration into why it is that certain statements of the paragraph's main idea are better or weaker than others. You'd also want to make sure your students understand that there is rarely only one way to state a given paragraph's main idea. Knowing this, they will more readily see that they could display their understanding of a paragraph's main idea (as operationalized by the state's test) by being able to compare the merits of alternative statements of that paragraph's central message.

But let's say that you don't think the statewide test demands enough from your 4th grade students. Let's say you believe that a 4th grader should be able to read a paragraph, perhaps one of several in an extended passage, and then figure out "from scratch" the main idea of any paragraph that happens to have one. And yes, you'd surely want to teach your students that not every paragraph has a main idea!

At any rate, although the state has operationalized this language arts aim in one way (maybe because of the cost-savings to be gained from a large-scale test that uses multiple-choice items), you decide to operationalize this main-idea reading skill in a different way, a way that suits your own instructional preferences. You decide to have your students read a paragraph, then write a single sentence that satisfactorily reflects the paragraph's central message. In fact, you decide to develop your own test of students' main-idea skills and administer it at both mid-year and near the close of the school year. Your test presents students with several multiparagraph passages, asks students to read each passage in its entirety, and then, for each paragraph that you designate, to write one well-worded sentence that suitably captures each designated paragraph's main idea. If any designated paragraph does not have a main idea, your students must say so in writing.

Think about how this different way of operationalizing the curricular aim would require different instructional activities. For instance, you'd need to help your 4th graders analyze paragraphs to determine if there is a main idea. Then, for paragraphs containing a main idea, you'd need to provide guidance and practice related to isolating the paragraph's central message from its supporting details so that students could learn how to produce pithy paraphrases. If you had used the state's multiple-choice test as your guide, these obviously sensible approaches might not have occurred to you—and might not have seemed (or been) necessary for your students to demonstrate "mastery."

What we learn from this example is that the same curricular aim, when operationalized differently, often requires dissimilar instructional approaches. For an additional illustration, take a look at Figure 2.2, which shows a typical 7th grade mathematics benchmark, lists two different ways to assess the benchmark's mastery, and outlines the contrasting instructional activities that might proceed from each of these two testing tactics. The two assessment approaches shown in this figure are, of course, fairly simplistic, but I hope they illustrate that one's teaching tactics ought to flow directly from one's testing tactics.

Seeking Students' Generalizable Mastery

You may already have picked up on a potential pitfall associated with test-operationalized curricular goals: the possibility that teachers might end up teaching their students to master only one kind of test-operationalized curricular aim. This kind of tunnel-vision instructional approach would indeed seriously shortchange students.

Remember, a test represents *one way* of getting evidence that you can use to make an inference about a student's covert status with respect to a variable like the student's skill in comprehending the main ideas in paragraphs. Each assessment approach that's chosen to

---

2.2   **ONE BENCHMARK, TWO TESTING TACTICS, AND THEIR INSTRUCTIONAL IMPLICATIONS**

7th Grade Mathematics Benchmark: Students will be able to employ appropriate measures of central tendency (*mean, median,* and *mode*) when describing sets of numerical data.

Testing Tactic One

Given a brief written or oral description of a fictitious but realistic setting in which the central tendency of numerical data must be described, the student will write a one-word answer indicating whether a *mean, median,* or *mode* is the most appropriate way to represent the data's central tendency.

Instructional Implications: Students must first be taught the reasons that each measure of central tendency would be preferred over its two counterparts for describing particular sets of numerical data. Then students should be supplied with ample guided and independent practice in (1) reading and listening to descriptions of lifelike situations involving numerical data and (2) supplying the name of the best measure of central tendency for describing such data.

● ● ● ● ●

Testing Tactic Two

Students will be asked (1) to write a brief description for each of the following types of central-tendency measures: *mean, median,* and *mode,* then (2) supply one written "real-world" example, of the student's own choosing, in which each of these measures has been properly used.

Instructional Implications: As this testing tactic calls for students to restate a memorized definition of the mean, median, and mode, students would need to be provided with accurate definitions so that those definitions can be memorized. Then, because students will be asked to come up with an appropriate real-world example for each measure of central tendency, students should practice generating their own examples, which the teacher or other students could check for accuracy.

---

operationalize a curricular aim carries with it implications for instructional design. Typically, tests requiring students to answer *selected-response items* (items in which students select from two or more already-present choices) will require meaningfully different instructional approaches than will tests requiring students to answer *constructed-response items* (items in which students must generate their answers). Any teacher trying to have students display main-idea mastery in the form of both selected-response (the state's multiple-choice test) and constructed-response tests (the teacher's "generate main ideas from scratch" test) will need to take two dissimilar instructional approaches.

As a teacher, what you first need to figure out for any curricular aim is just what sort of *cognitive demand* will be imposed on students by any test that's being used to measure mastery of that curricular aim. A cognitive demand describes the intellectual activities in which a student must engage in order to be successful in dealing with the tasks contained in the particular kind of assessment. The critical question you need to ask yourself is this: "For students to truly master this curricular aim, what must be going on inside their heads?"

If you ask that question after considering different types of tests that could be used to measure a given content standard, you'll often find that the different types of tests impose different cognitive demands on students. We saw this to be true for the fourth-grade teacher who chose to measure students' main idea skills in a manner other than that used in a statewide test. Different assessments in that instance called for different instructional activities.

Clearly, teachers want to teach their students to master important cognitive skills in such a way that students' skill-mastery is *generalizable*. A student who possesses generalizable skill-mastery will be able to apply that mastery in all sorts of in-school and out-of-school settings. There is a real virtue, then, in employing diverse kinds of assessments. In other words, try to measure a student's skill-mastery in several ways, some requiring the student to generate a correct answer and some requiring the student to select a correct answer from an array of presented options. Make sure that some of your constructed-response tasks call for written responses and others call for oral responses. Use a kind of "mix and match" approach to educational testing so that you can get an accurate fix on your students' generalizable mastery. The more diverse the assessment techniques that you adopt, the stronger the inference they will give you about the essence of the cognitive demands those varied tests are imposing on your students. Accordingly, the instruction you design will incorporate a variety of different explanations, different kinds of modeling, and different sorts of practice exercises.

Take another look at the three ways of measuring main idea comprehension identified on page 21. If I were promoting my own students' main-idea mastery, I'd initially consider all three assessment tactics to help me get a better handle on the true cognitive demand of this skill. Then I'd incorporate all three assessment-grounded instructional approaches into my teaching, obliging my students to show me the various ways that they could pull out the main idea from any main-idea–containing paragraph they happened to encounter. This is how generalized skill-mastery is born.

Of course, there are some skills for which it is difficult to come up with genuinely diverse assessment tactics. For instance, if I wanted my students to be able to write accurate direction-giving essays in order to show a friend how to walk from Place X to Place Y, my chief approach to test-based operationalizing of this skill would revolve around a written test of students' direction-giving skill—some form of a written direction-giving essay. Multiple-choice items, matching items, or True-False items simply wouldn't fill the bill in this instance, either to help me better understand the skill's essence or as practice exercises to help my students become more skilled writers of direction-giving essays.

Most of the time, though, you will find that it is possible to come up with substantively different ways of measuring a student's mastery of individual content standards. Those diverse assessment tactics will not only help you better understand what each content standard is really seeking, but will also provide you with instructional cues about how best to get your students to master each content standard in a generalizable manner.

Teaching Toward Test-Represented Targets, Not Toward Tests

As you've seen, educational tests can be used to clarify a curricular outcome by exemplifying a way of using students' overt performances to make inferences about students' covert status regarding sought-for knowledge, skills, or affect. Thus, a test functions as a representation of the educational variable to be sought instructionally.

Let me say it again: A test is only a *representation,* meaning that teachers must aim their instruction not at the tests, but toward the skill, knowledge, or affect that those tests represent. This is such an important point that I dare not race forward without pounding my measurement tom-tom for just a moment more. Far too many folks in education, often those who know the least about testing, ascribe far too much importance to educational tests. Rather than seeing tests as a means to a fairly accurate fix on an unseen educational variable, these people believe that tests actually *are* the educational variable being promoted. In short, they reify educational tests as the true target of their instructional efforts. The idea that tests are instructional targets, wrongheaded as it is, is unfortunately bolstered by many high-stakes statewide testing programs. Preoccupation with test scores becomes so profound that many teachers and administrators mistakenly succumb to the belief that increased test scores *are* appropriate educational targets. They're not.

Educators must recognize that tests are sometimes fallible tools and that the only legitimate application of these tools is to help us determine a student's status with respect to a significant educational variable. When this point is clear, most teachers will try to aim their instruction toward what a test represents rather than toward the test itself. Diverse types of tests will usually incline teachers to do just this.

INSTRUCTIONALLY FOCUSED TESTING TIPS

• Clarify the nature of any curricular aim by analyzing the assessments intended to measure students' attainment of that aim.

• Clarify your own understanding of a curricular aim by considering the various ways that students' achievement of that aim might be assessed.

• Promote your students' mastery of any important curricular aim by employing diverse assessment approaches to measure that aim.

• Teach toward the skills or knowledge a test represents, not toward the test itself.

Recommended Resources

Anderson, L. W., & Krathwohl, D. R. (Eds.). (2001). *A taxonomy for learning, teaching, and assessing: A revision of Bloom's taxonomy of educational objectives*. New York: Longman.

Jacobs, H. H. (Program Consultant). (1991). *Curriculum mapping: Charting the course for content* [Videotape]. Alexandria, VA: Association for Supervision and Curriculum Development.

Kendall, J. S., & Marzano, R. J. (2000). *Content knowledge: A compendium of standards and benchmarks for K–12 education* (3rd ed.). Alexandria, VA: Association for Supervision and Curriculum Development; and Aurora, CO: McREL.

Ohanian, S. (1999). *One size fits few: The folly of educational standards*. Portsmouth, NH: Heinemann.

Popham, W. J. (Program Consultant). (2000). *Test preparation: The wrong way/right way* [Videotape]. Los Angeles: IOX Assessment Associates.

3

Too Many
Testing Targets

TEACHERS WANT TO FIND OUT WHAT'S GOING ON INSIDE STUDENTS' HEADS. PUT-ting it a bit more formally, teachers want to make inferences about the nature of their students' skills, knowledge, and affect. And that's the precise point at which the integral relationship between curricu-lum and assessment takes center stage. You see, testing doesn't take place in a vacuum. More specifically, testing doesn't take place in a curriculum-free vacuum. Typically, teachers test students to get a fix on their students' status with respect to those cognitive or affective targets that have been laid out in a prescribed curriculum. More often than not, therefore, teachers find themselves trying to "test what's in the curriculum."

As a result, most educators today also end up trying to solve an essentially insolvable problem: how to satisfactorily assess students' mastery of too many curricular aims imposed "from above." There's an oft-uttered saying that you can't make a silk purse out of a sow's ear. The gist of the saying's message, of course, is that if you are given unsuitable raw material, it's impossible to transform that raw material into something spectacular. When teachers are informed that they should promote their students' mastery of a huge number of state-stipulated or district-stipulated curricular goals, many teachers actu-ally try to do so. Unfortunately, that's almost always a mistake.

Assessment and curriculum are *not* a pair of isolated enclaves, each functioning happily without any reference to the other. Teachers ought to test what students ought to learn and, yes, what's set forth in a curriculum should be the dominant determiner of the sorts of classroom tests that teachers give to their students. But too many educators reckon that assessment programs can blossom irrespective of the curricula from which they spring. State-level testing does not occur apart from the test-developers' attention to state curricula. And, just as surely, classroom-level testing should not occur apart from a teacher's attention to curricular considerations. Thus, if teachers are dealing with a sow's-ear curriculum, they'll never be able to create silk-purse assessments. It's important, therefore, to know what you can do if you find yourself forced to cope with a curriculum prescription that contains too many pills in its bottle. In this chapter, I'll look at the origins of the problem and then offer my recommendations on how to solve it in your own classroom.

Standards-Based Reform

A half-century ago, almost every U.S. state set out an officially approved curriculum for its schools. This authorized curriculum, sometimes called a "state curriculum syllabus," identified the knowledge and skills that the state's teachers were supposed to promote at different grade levels (or grade ranges) and in most subjects. Frankly, few educators paid much attention to those curricular documents. State curricular syllabi nestled quietly in teachers' desk drawers, rarely to be opened.

In the 1990s, many educational policymakers began to proclaim the virtues of *standards-based reform* as a new strategy to reform public schools. Here's how it was intended to work. First, a group of experienced teachers and curriculum specialists in each state met to stake out a set of challenging content standards for each grade level, or for grade ranges, in all key subjects. (In most instances, these collections of content standards were dead ringers for yesteryear's curricular syllabi.) Then, a statewide test was either selected or constructed to assess students' mastery of those content standards. Finally, students' test performances were employed to identify the schools (and teachers) whose students were achieving high scores or low scores. High-scoring schools were regarded as winners; low-scoring schools were regarded as losers.

The underlying strategy of standards-based reforms rested solidly on the proposition that by administering standards-based tests annually to students at selected grade levels, the state's teachers would be spurred to effectively promote students' content-standard mastery (as reflected by higher test scores). Those higher test scores would, of course, signify improved student mastery of the state's challenging content standards.

Unfortunately, there turned out to be several significant short-comings in the way that the educational officials in most states tried to implement standards-based reform. For one thing, typically, the quality of the alignment between state-approved content standards and state-approved achievement tests has been very weak. Rather than devote scarce educational funds to the development of customized tests based exclusively on a state's curriculum, many states simply chose to use an off-the-shelf standardized achievement test. Such tests were selected despite the fact that many of the state's approved content standards appeared to be addressed by only one or two items in those off-the-shelf tests. And, worse, in some instances there were state content standards that weren't measured by even one item in those already-built standardized achievement tests.

Rarely, however, do even *custom-built* statewide standards-based tests include sufficient numbers of items to provide evidence of a student's status with respect to the mastery of *particular* content standards. That's a serious shortcoming, because unless teachers, students, and parents can determine which content standards are being mastered and which ones are not, then standards-based reform is doomed to be little more than an attractive but meaningless bit of rhetoric.

You see, if we don't know which content standards have been successfully promoted, then teachers can't tell whether particular parts of their instructional programs have been effective or ineffective. But there's an equally serious deficiency with most of today's standards-based reform efforts, and that problem lies in the curricular corner-stones of this entire reform strategy: *the content standards themselves.*

Typically, the people who carve out the content standards for any given state are a group of experienced educators, perhaps 20–30 such individuals, who have been selected for the task because of their expertise in the subject areas for which the content standards are being identified. For instance, the Content Standards Committee of 25 educators in State *X* who have been directed to identify the knowledge and skills in *science* that State *X* students in grades 4–8 should master is typically composed of science-education *specialists.*

Specialists, as we all know, tend to love their specialties. That's the strength *and* the weakness of the way that most states have identified their content standards. When subject-matter specialists are asked to isolate what students need to know about their specialty, the specialists' response will almost always be "Everything!" In other words, because the people who take part in the identification of content standards typically revere their subject fields, they often identify all the knowledge and all the skills that they *wish* well-taught children at a given age would possess.

The net effect of this kind of *wish-list* curricular thinking is that, in most states, the number of content standards officially approved for most subjects is enormous. These wish-list content standards simply aren't teachable in the instructional time available to the classroom teachers. It's equally unrealistic to think that these litanies of content standards can be satisfactorily assessed by an annual state-wide test of 50–60 items per subject area. In most instances, only a small proportion of these lengthy lists of state-approved content standards are measured at all, even by one puny item.

Think of the teachers in states where wish-list content standards abound. You can be certain that there is nothing even approximating total measurement of these standards. Unquestionably, therefore, these teachers will face some absurd choices. The educational-reform strategy in place has likely attracted substantial political support in high places. (Politicians typically revel in rallying behind the "promotion of high standards.") Moreover, most citizens joyfully applaud the merits of any accountability strategy aimed at promoting students' mastery of "demanding" content standards. And yet, the two most important components of this accountability strategy typically malfunction. The content standards are far too numerous to teach, and far, far too numerous to test. The culminating high-stakes tests used to assess students' mastery of those standards don't actually measure those standards and, worse, don't help teachers make defensible instructional decisions.

Coping with Unrealistic Curricular Demands

Teachers who are being asked to promote their students' mastery of an unwieldy array of state-sanctioned content standards, and to do so without receiving test results that reveal students' standard-by-standard status, are in an untenable instructional situation. But even though such expectations may be unrealistic, those expectations are still very real. And there are adverse consequences for teachers who fall short. How, then, should teachers cope?

My advice is to select a coping strategy, given your available alternatives, that is most likely to benefit your students. One popular but unwise response to a rambling, excessive set of standards-based expectations—an aiming-for-a-silk-purse response that most certainly *won't* help students—is to try to "cover" all the state-stipulated standards. Shallow coverage, almost by definition, will rarely lead to deep understanding, especially when teachers must race on to tomorrow's content standards before students have the chance to master today's.

It would be far better, of course, if a state's policymakers would realize that they've given teachers too much to teach (and test) in the time available, and, after some serious curricular soul-searching, they would attach estimates of importance to their too-long sets of content standards. Thereafter, the state's teachers could determine which curricular outcomes were really the most imperative to foster. What's more, a more modest number of super-significant content standards would make it possible to create standards-based tests that could report students' results on a standard-by-standard basis, thus providing the explicit standards-mastery information that teachers could use to refine or revise their instructional approaches.

However, many teachers will find that their own state's standards-based reform strategy has not been improved along these lines. So, given this sort of unhappy situation, my best advice to teachers is to *prioritize for yourself.* Either on your own or (even better) in collegial teams, review the complete set of content standards for which you are responsible, and set your own priorities.

Here's how I think the prioritizing game should be played. First, consider every single content standard on the state- or district-approved list for the subject area or areas in which you teach. For *each* content standard in your subject, assign one of three ratings:

• *Essential.* It is absolutely necessary for my students to have mastered this content standard by the end of my instruction.
• *Highly desirable.* It very important for my students to have mastered this content standard by the end of my instruction.
• *Desirable.* If possible, I would like my students to have mastered this content standard by the end of my instruction.

After you've *rated* all the content standards, then you need to *rank* only the ones that you already rated as "essential." Rank all of those essential content standards from most important (#1 on your list) to next most important (#2), and so on. Then, design your instruction so that you can do a thorough and effective job of promoting your students' mastery of as many of the highest prioritized content standards as you can promote in the instructional time you have available. Naturally, you'd like to have your students learn as many good things as they possibly can, so you'll also want to give at least some instructional attention to those content standards you regarded as "highly desirable" and "desirable." But any such instructional attention need not be as extensive as the instructional attention you devote to your highest-priority essential content standards. Remember, what you're trying to do is to get your students to master the knowledge and skills that, in your professional judgment, are the "very most important."

And what about assessment? Well, although we've seen that total measurement of innumerable content standards is impossible, especially if one is trying to get a fix on students' per-standard mastery, it is definitely possible to assess a *more limited number* of high-priority content standards. And that's just what you need to do.

In the last chapter, I pointed out how a somewhat vague content standard can be operationalized by the assessment (or, preferably, by the multiple assessments) employed to measure mastery of that vague content standard. Consistent with that advice, what you need to do is come up with suitable assessments for *each* of the high-priority content standards you've decided to tackle instructionally. The assessments you choose will typically lead you to better instructional decisions because of the increased clarity that those "operationalizing" assessments will provide. Moreover, if you use pre-assessments to determine what your students already know and can do, you'll be better able to choose suitable instructional activities for those students. At the end of your instruction, of course, you'll be able to get a test-based estimate of how well your students have mastered each high-priority content standard that you've set out to pursue. Additionally, if you use any sort of less-formal *en route* assessments, perhaps you'll find that your students have mastered some content standards more rapidly than you'd anticipated, thus enabling you to move on to your next high-priority standard and, ultimately, give instructional attention to other important standards that did not make your initial cut.

Counteracting the Myth of Total Measurement

It is impossible, in real schools, to assess students' attainment of all the lovely curricular aims we'd like those students to accomplish. "Total measurement" is a myth. Moreover, the pretense that a lengthy list of content standards can somehow be accurately measured breeds a corollary myth of "total instruction." It is just as silly to think that teachers can effectively promote students' mastery of seemingly endless content standards as it is to think that all those content standards can be properly assessed.

Prioritizing offers a reasonable way out of this instructional dilemma. (To my mind, it is the only way out of this bind.) Teachers need to prioritize a set of content standards so they can identify the content standards at which they will devote powerful, thoroughgoing instruction, and then they need to *formally and systematically* assess students' mastery of only those high-priority content standards. Time permitting, instructional attention to other, lower-priority content standards could certainly be worked in. And other, less systematic assessments could also be used to gauge students' mastery of those same lower-priority content standards.

Some might object to the prioritization strategy I have recommended here because it seems to suggest that a teacher should be doing *less* with students—should be focusing on *fewer* curricular aims. To such criticism, I reply that there's a whopping big difference between content standards that are *simply sought* and content standards that are *truly taught*. Indeed, when teachers unthinkingly set out to seek student mastery of so many curricular outcomes, what is sought will, in fact, rarely be taught. The more ground that teachers try to cover, the less likely it is they'll be able to help students gain deep understandings and facility with complex skills. That's what "challenging" content standards call for, and that's what everyone really wants.

I'm suggesting that teachers, and the administrators they report to, need to be honest about what's instructionally accomplishable in a finite amount of teaching time. And that kind of honesty leads me to encourage you to do a serious prioritizing job on *any* curricular aims that have been officially tossed into your lap. If the pressure to "cover all content standards" is really severe, then you may wish to give *really* rapid-fire treatment to the whole set of content standards, but give your genuine instructional and assessment attention to only the curricular aims you believe to be truly of the highest significance.

My proposed prioritization strategy was initially spawned in response to ill-conceived, state reform strategies built around excessively lengthy lists of content standards. Please recognize, however, that this prioritization strategy can work just as effectively when teachers are trying to figure out how best to organize their own instruction and to evaluate its effectiveness. After all, even if a teacher had no official state-imposed content standards to wrestle with, that teacher would still have to decide what to emphasize instructionally and what to emphasize from an assessment perspective. There's lots of stuff to teach, and there's lots of stuff to test. Teachers will do a better job for their students if they devote serious effort to identifying the most significant things that can be taught in the time available. Then those high-priority curricular aims can be well taught and well tested. A prioritization strategy is clearly predicated on a less-is-more approach to teaching and testing. And it works!

A Labyrinth of Labels

Now I want to change my focus for just a bit. In this chapter, I've tried to tackle a curricular problem that is causing today's teachers a heap of instructional and assessment headaches. The essence of my message is that excessive curricular aspirations can make instructionally sensible assessment impossible. Thus, when teachers are tussling with their own testing issues, it's rare that curriculum considerations aren't involved.

And because that's so, I want to close out the chapter with a brief treatment of several curriculum-related labels that today's classroom teachers are almost sure to encounter. As you'll see, teachers who are baffled by the meaning of these labels will rarely be able to make the best curricular *or* assessment decisions.

In the previous chapter, we saw that there are lots of ways to describe curricular aims: goals, objectives, expectancies, benchmarks, learning outcomes, and so on. Today's most popular label is *content standards*. In the No Child Left Behind Act, curricular aims are described as *academic content standards*. Typically, classroom teachers pursue content standards stipulated by state or district authorities, although many teachers sometimes add on a few noncompulsory content standards that they personally regard as worthwhile.

There is one strong possibility of semantic confusion these days, however, and that stems from the use of another descriptive label: *performance standards.** A performance standard refers to the required level of proficiency students are expected to display when they have mastered a content standard. For example, if a content standard calls for a student to write a coherent paragraph, a performance standard indicates *how well* that paragraph must be written. Or, if a content standard focuses on the student's acquisition of knowledge—say, knowing the definitions of 50 biological terms—a performance standard describes *how many* of the 50 terms a student would need to know in order to have "mastered" the content standard. Thirty-five terms? Forty terms? Forty-five?

---

*The authors of the No Child Left Behind Act used the term *academic achievement standards* rather than "performance standards." As the nation's educators become more familiar with NCLB requirements, this phrase may become more widely used. However, for the time being, I'm going to stick with the more commonly employed terminology, namely, *performance standards*.

A content standard without an accompanying performance standard is like a play without a final act. You can't tell what the content standard really signifies until you know how students' mastery of it will be assessed and, thereafter, until you know what sort of performance standard has been set on that assessment. Even the loftiest content standard can be transformed into a trifling expectation if the bar is set very low. Likewise, a trivial content standard can become a challenging, praiseworthy expectation when it's accompanied by a super-stringent performance standard. For instance, if elementary school students were to be able to name the capitals of all 50 states (the content standard), you could set a mandatory 100 percent correct level (the performance standard) for proficient performance. The result would be a tough task for students, even though the task deals with a rather trivial curricular aim.

Increasingly, U.S. educators are building performance standards along the lines of the descriptive categories used in the National Assessment Educational Progress (NAEP), a test administered periodically under the auspices of the federal government. NAEP results permit students' performances in participating states to be compared, so that it can be seen which states' students outperform which other states' students. (Given Americans' abiding preoccupation with winners and losers, it's surprising that no one has thought to report NAEP results in newspapers' sports sections.) At any rate, since 1990, NAEP results have been described in four performance categories: *advanced, proficient, basic,* and *below basic.* Most of the 50 states now use those four categories or labels quite similar to them. For example, if students were taking a statewide examination consisting of 65 multiple-choice items, the performance standards for that test could be set by deciding how many of the 65 items must be answered correctly for a student to be classified as *advanced,* how many items for *proficient,* and so on.

My point is that performance standards are malleable, and you never know what something like "basic" means until you read the fine-print description of that level of performance. For example, the No Child Left Behind Act calls for states to establish at least three levels of academic achievement standards (*advanced, proficient,* and *basic*) and to demonstrate, over time, state-decreed increases in the proportion of students deemed "proficient" or above. Because the thrust of NCLB is to get *all* students to be proficient or advanced, the legislation describes the *basic* level as "the progress of lower-achieving children toward mastering the proficient and advanced levels of achievement." However, each state is allowed to define "proficient" in its own way. And because there are significant negative sanctions for schools that fail to get enough students to score at the proficient levels on NCLB tests, in some states there have been *remarkably* lenient levels of "proficiency" established.

Clearly, because the two kinds of standards (content and performance) have such distinctive purposes, teachers need to avoid the confusion that's likely to arise when one simply refers to "standards" without a preceding adjective. I encourage you to avoid talking about "high standards" or "challenging standards" because, as you've just seen, if we really want our students to accomplish worthwhile things, we'll need high-level content standards accompanied by high-level performance standards.

INSTRUCTIONALLY FOCUSED TESTING TIPS

- Learn which content standards are required by your state or district.
- Determine if those content standards are accompanied by performance standards.
- Prioritize any officially sanctioned content standards.
- Systematically assess only the high-priority content standards.
- Give major instructional attention to only the high-priority content standards.

Recommended Resources

Falk, B. (2000). *The heart of the matter: Using standards and assessment to learn.* Westport, CT: Heinemann.

Jacobs, H. H. (Program Consultant). (1991). *Curriculum mapping: Charting the course for content* [Videotape]. Alexandria, VA: Association for Supervision and Curriculum Development.

Kohn, A. (1999). *The schools our children deserve: Moving beyond traditional classrooms and "tougher standards."* Port Chester, NY: National Professional Resources, Inc.

Kohn, A. (Program Consultant). (2000). *Beyond the standards movement: Defending quality education in an age of test scores* [Videotape]. Port Chester, NY: National Professional Resources, Inc.

Linn, R. L. (2000, March). Assessments and accountability. *Educational Researcher, 29*(2), 4–16.

Validity, Reliability, and Bias

4

FEW IF ANY SIGNIFICANT ASSESSMENT CONCEPTS ARE COMPLETELY UNRELATED TO a teacher's instructional decision making. To prove it, in this chapter I'm going to trot out three of the most important measurement ideas—validity, reliability, and assessment bias—and then show you how each of them bears directly on the instructional choices that teachers must make.

These three measurement concepts are just about as important as measurement concepts can get. Although teachers need not be measurement experts, basic *assessment literacy* is really a professional obligation, and this chapter will unpack some key terminology and clarify what you really need to know.

It is impossible to be assessment literate without possessing at least a rudimentary understanding of validity, reliability, and assessment bias. They are the foundation for trustworthy inferences. As teachers, we can't guarantee that any test-based inference we make is accurate, but a basic understanding of validity, reliability, and assessment bias increases the odds in our favor. And the more we can trust our test-based inferences, the better our insight into students and the better our test-based decisions. Also, in this age of accountability, the fallout from invalid inferences could be invalid conclusions by administrators, by parents, and by politicians that you and your school are doing a sub-par job.

Validity

At the very apex of all measurement concepts is the notion of *validity*. Indeed, the concept of validity almost always finds its way into any conversation about educational testing. Well, in the next few paragraphs you'll learn that *there is no such thing as a valid test.*

The Validity of Inferences

The reason that there's no such thing as a valid test is quite straightforward: It's not the test itself that can be valid or invalid but, rather, the *inference* that's based on a student's test performance. Is the score-based inference that a teacher has made a valid one? Or, in contrast, has the teacher made a score-based inference that's invalid? All validity analysis should center on the test-based inference, rather than on the test itself. Let's see how this inference-making process works and, thereafter, how educators can determine if their own score-based inferences are valid or not.

You'll remember from Chapter 1 that educators use educational tests to secure overt evidence about covert variables, such as a student's ability to spell, read, or perform arithmetic operations. Well, even though teachers can look at students' overt test scores, they're still obliged to come up with the interpretation about what those test scores mean. If the interpretation is *accurate*, we say that the teacher has arrived at a *valid* test-based inference. If the interpretation is *inaccurate*, then the teacher's test-based inference is *invalid*.

You might be wondering, why is this author making such a big fuss about whether it's the test or the test-based inference that's valid? Well, if a *test* can be labeled as valid or invalid, then it is surely true that assessment accuracy resides in the test itself. By this logic, that test would yield unerringly accurate information no matter how it's used or to whom it's administered. For instance, let's say a group of

Ethiopian test-developers have created a brand new science test for children. Because the test was developed by Ethiopians in Ethiopia, the test items and text passages are in Amharic, the official language of that nation. Now, if that test were administered to Ethiopian children, the scores would probably yield valid inferences about these children's science skills and knowledge. But if it were administered to English-speaking children in a Kansas school district, any test-based inferences about those children's science skills and knowledge would be altogether inaccurate. The test itself would yield accurate interpretations in one setting with one group of test-takers, yet inaccurate interpretations in another setting, with another group of test-takers. It is the score-based *inference* that is accurate in Ethiopia, but inaccurate in Kansas. It is not the *test*.

The same risk of invalid inferences applies in any testing situation where factors interfere with test-takers' ability to demonstrate what they know and can do. For example, consider a 14-year-old gifted writer recently arrived from El Salvador who cannot express herself in English; a trigonometry student with cerebral palsy who cannot control a pencil well enough to draw sine curves; a 6th grader who falls asleep 5 minutes into the test and only completes 10 of the 50 test items. Even superlative tests, when used in these circumstances or other settings where extraneous factors can diminish the accuracy of score-based inferences, will often lead to mistaken interpretations. If you recognize that educational tests do not possess some sort of inherent accurate or inaccurate essence, then you will more likely realize that assessment validity rests on *human judgment* about the inferences derived from students' test performances. And human judgment is sometimes faulty.

The task of measurement experts who deal professionally with assessment validity, then, is to assemble evidence that a particular score-based inference made in a particular context is valid. With tests used in large-scale assessments (such as a statewide, high school graduation test), the experts' quest is to assemble a collection of evidence that will support the validity of the test-based inferences that are drawn from the test. Rarely does a single "validity study" supply sufficiently compelling evidence regarding the validity of any test-based inference. In most cases, to determine whether any given type of score-based inference is on the mark, it is necessary to consider the collection of validity evidence in a number of studies.

Three Varieties of Validity Evidence

There are three kinds of validity evidence sanctioned by the relevant professional organizations: (1) *criterion-related evidence,* (2) *construct-related evidence,* and (3) *content-related evidence.* Each type, usually collected via some sort of investigation or analytic effort, contributes to the conclusion that a test is yielding data that will support valid inferences. Typically, such investigations are funded by test-makers before they bring their off-the-shelf product to the market. In other instances, validity studies are required by state authorities prior to test-selection or prior to "launching" a test they've commissioned. We'll take a brief peek at each evidence type, paying particular attention to the one that should most concern a classroom teacher.

Before we do that, though, I need to call your attention to an important distinction to keep in mind when dealing with educational tests: the difference between an *achievement test* and an *aptitude test.* An achievement test is intended to measure the skills and knowledge that a student currently possesses in a particular subject area. For instance, the social studies test in the Metropolitan Achievement Tests is intended to supply an idea of students' social studies skills and knowledge. Classroom tests that teachers construct to see how much their students have learned are other examples of achievement tests. In contrast, an aptitude test is intended to help predict a student's future performance, typically in a subsequent academic setting. The best examples of this test type are the widely used ACT and SAT, which are supposed to predict how well high school students will perform when they get to college.

As you'll read in Chapter 9, there are many times when these two supposedly different kinds of educational tests actually function in an almost identical manner. Nevertheless, it's an important terminology difference that you need to know, and it comes into particular focus regarding the first type of validity evidence, which we're going to examine right now.

Criterion-related evidence of validity. This kind of validity concerns whether aptitude tests really predict what they were intended to predict. Investigators directing a study to collect criterion-related evidence of validity simply administer the aptitude test to high school students and then follow those students during their college careers to see if the predictions based on the aptitude test were accurately predictive of the criterion. In the case of the SAT or ACT, the criterion would be those students' college grade-point averages. If the relationship between the predictive test scores and the college grades is strong, then this finding constitutes criterion-related evidence supporting the validity of score-based inferences about high school students' probable academic success in college.

Clearly, classroom teachers do not have the time to collect criterion-referenced evidence of validity, especially about aptitude tests. That's a task better left to assessment specialists. Few teachers I know have ever been mildly tempted to create an aptitude test, much less collect criterion-related validity evidence regarding that test.

Construct-related evidence of validity. Most measurement specialists regard construct-related evidence as the most comprehensive form of validity evidence because, in a sense, it covers *all* forms of validity evidence. To explain what construct-related evidence of validity is, I need to provide a short description of how it is collected.

The first step is identifying some sort of *hypothetical construct*, another term for the covert variable sought. As we've learned, this can be something as exotic as a person's "depression potential" or as straightforward as a student's skill in written composition. Next, based on the understanding of the nature of the hypothetical construct identified, a test to measure that construct is developed, and a study is designed to help determine whether the test does, in fact, measure the construct. The form of such studies can vary substantially, but they are all intended to supply empirical evidence that the test is behaving in the way it is supposed to behave.

Here's what I hope is a helpful example. One kind of construct-related validity study is called a *differential population* investigation. The validity investigator identifies two groups of people who are almost certain to differ in the degree to which they possess the construct being measured. For instance, let's say a new test is being investigated that deals with college students' mathematical skills. The investigator locates 25 college math majors and another 25 college students who haven't taken a math course since 9th grade. The investigator then predicts that when all 50 students take the new test, the math whizzes will blow away the math nonwhizzes. The 50 students take the test, and that's just the way things turn out. The investigator's prediction has been confirmed by empirical evidence, so this represents construct-related evidence that, yes, the new test really does measure college students' math skills.

There are a host of other approaches to the collection of construct-related validity evidence, and some are quite exotic. As a practical matter, though, busy classroom teachers don't have time to be carrying out such investigations. Still, I hope it's clear that because all attempts to collect validity evidence really do relate to the existence of an unseen educational variable, most measurement specialists believe that it's accurate to characterize every validity study as some form of a construct-related validity study.

Content-related evidence of validity. This third kind of validity evidence is also (finally) the kind that classroom teachers might wish to collect. Briefly put, this form of evidence tries to establish that a test's items satisfactorily reflect the content the test is supposed to represent. And the chief method of carrying out such content-related validity studies is to rely on *human judgment.*

I'll start with an example that shows how to collect content-related evidence of validity for a district-built or school-built test. Let's say that the English teachers in a high school are trying to build a new test to assess students' mastery of four language arts content standards—the four standards from their state-approved set that they, as a group, have decided are the most important. They decide to assess students' mastery of each of these content standards through a 32-item test, with 8 items devoted to each of the 4 standards.

The team of English teachers creates a draft version of their new test and then sets off in pursuit of content-related evidence of the draft test's validity. They assemble a review panel of a dozen individuals, half of them English teachers from another school and the other half parents who majored or minored in English in college. The review panel meets for a couple of hours on a Saturday morning, and its members make individual judgments about each of the 32 items, all of which have been designated as primarily assessing one of the 4 content standards. The judgments required of the review panel all revolve around the four content standards that the items are supposedly measuring. For example, all panelists might be asked to review the content standards and then respond to the following question for each of the 32 test items:

> Will a student's response to this item help teachers determine whether a student has mastered the designated content standard that the item is intended to assess?
>
> _____ Yes   _____ No   _____ Uncertain

After the eight items linked to a particular content standard have been judged by members of the review panel, the panelists might be asked to make the following sort of judgment:

> Considering the complete set of eight items intended to measure this designated content standard, indicate how accurately you

believe a teacher will be able to judge a student's content-standard mastery based on the students' response to these eight items.

_____ Very Accurately   _____ Somewhat Accurately

_____ Not Too Accurately

It's true that the process I've just described represents a considerable effort. That's okay for state-developed, district-developed, or school-developed tests . . . but how might individual teachers go about collecting content-related evidence of validity for their own, individually created classroom tests? First, I'd suggest doing so only for very important tests, such as midterm or final exams. Collecting content-related evidence of validity does take time, and it can be a ton of trouble, so do it judiciously. Second, you can get by with a small number of validity judges, perhaps a colleague or two or a parent or two. Remember that the essence of the judgments you'll be asking others to make revolves around whether your tests satisfactorily represent the content they are supposed to represent. The more "representative" your tests, the more likely it is that any of your test-based inferences will be valid.

Ideally, of course, individual teachers should construct classroom tests from a content-related validity perspective. What this means, in a practical manner, is that teachers who develop their own tests should be continually attentive to the curricular aims each test is supposed to represent. It's advisable to keep a list of the relevant objectives on hand and create specific items to address those objectives. If teachers think seriously about the content-representativeness of the tests they are building, those tests are more likely to yield valid score-based inferences.

Figure 4.1 presents a summing-up graphic depiction of how students' mastery of a content standard is measured by a test . . . and the three kinds of validity evidence that can be collected to support the validity of a test-based inference about students' mastery of the content standard.

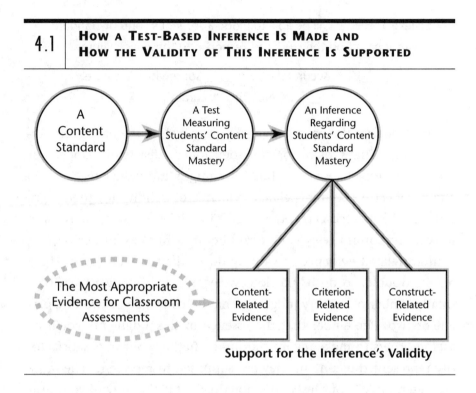

4.1 HOW A TEST-BASED INFERENCE IS MADE AND
HOW THE VALIDITY OF THIS INFERENCE IS SUPPORTED

In contrast to measurement specialists, who are often called on to collect all three varieties of validity evidence (especially for important tests), classroom teachers rarely collect any validity evidence at all. But it is possible for teachers to collect content-related evidence of validity, the type most useful in the classroom, without a Herculean effort. When it comes to the most important of your classroom exams, it might be worthwhile for you to do so.

Validity in the Classroom

Now, how does the concept of assessment validity relate to a teacher's instructional decisions? Well, it's pretty clear that if you come up with incorrect conclusions about your students' status regarding important educational variables, including their mastery of particular content standards, you'll be more likely to make unsound instructional decisions. The better fix you get on your students' status (especially regarding such unseen variables as their cognitive skills), the more defensible your instructional decisions will be. Valid assessment-based inferences about students don't always translate into brilliant instructional decisions; however, *invalid* assessment-based inferences about students almost always lead to dim-witted or, at best, misguided instructional decisions.

Let me illustrate the sorts of unsound instructional decisions that teachers can make when they base those decisions on invalid test-based inferences. Unfortunately, I can readily draw on my own class-room experience to do so. When I first began teaching in that small, eastern Oregon high school, one of my assigned classes was senior English. As I thought about that class in the summer months leading up to my first salaried teaching position, I concluded that I wanted those 12th grade English students to leave my class "being good writ-ers." In other words, I wanted to make sure that if any of my students (whom I'd not yet met) went on to college, they'd be able to write decent essays, reports, and so on.

Well, when I taught that English course, I was pretty pleased with my students' progress in being able to write. As the year went by, they were doing better and better on the exams I employed to judge their writing skills. My instructional decisions seemed to be sensible, because the 32 students in my English class were scoring well on my exams. The only trouble was . . . all of my exams contained only multiple-choice items about the mechanics of writing. With suitable shame, I now confess that *I never assessed my students' writing skills by asking them to write anything!* What a cluck.

I never altered my instruction, not even a little, because I used my students' scores on multiple-choice tests to arrive at an inference that "they were learning how to write." Based on my students' measured progress, my instruction was pretty spiffy and didn't need to be changed. An invalid test-based inference had led me to an unsound instructional decision, namely, providing mechanics-only writing instruction. If I had known back then how to garner content-related evidence of validity for my multiple-choice tests about the mechanics of writing, I'd probably have figured out that my selected-response exams weren't truly able to help me reach reasonable inferences about my students' constructed-response abilities to write essays, reports, and so on.

You will surely not be as much of an assessment illiterate as I was during my first few years of teaching, but you do need to look at the content of your exams to see if they can contribute to the kinds of inferences about your students that you truly need to make.

Reliability

Reliability is another much-talked-about measurement concept. It's a major concern to the developers of large-scale tests, who usually devote substantial energy to its calculation. A test's reliability refers to its *consistency*. In fact, if you were never to utter the word "reliability" again, preferring to employ "consistency" instead, you could still live a rich and satisfying life.

Three Kinds of Reliability

As was true with validity, assessment reliability also comes in three flavors. However, the three ways of thinking about an assessment instrument's consistency are really quite strikingly different, and it's important that educators understand the distinctions.

Stability reliability. This first kind of reliability concerns the consistency with which a test measures something over time. For instance, if students took a standardized achievement test on the first day of a month and, without any intervening instruction regarding what the test measured, took the same test again at the end of the month, would students' scores be about the same?

Alternate-form reliability. The crux of this second kind of reliability is fairly evident from its name. If there are two supposedly equivalent forms of a test, do those two forms actually yield student scores that are pretty similar? If Jamal scored well on Form *A*, will Jamal also score well on Form *B*? Clearly, alternate-form reliability only comes into play when there are two or more forms of a test that are supposed to be doing the same assessment job.

Internal consistency reliability. This third kind of reliability focuses on the consistency of the items within a test. Do all of the test's items appear to be doing the same kind of measurement job? For internal consistency reliability to make much sense, of course, a test should be aimed at a single overall variable—for instance, a student's reading comprehension. If a language arts test tried to simultaneously measure a student's reading comprehension, spelling ability, and punctuation skills, then it wouldn't make much sense to see if the test's items were functioning in a similar manner. After all, because three distinct things are being measured, the test's items *shouldn't* be functioning in a homogeneous manner.

Do you see how the three forms of reliability, although all related to aspects of a test's consistency, are conceptually dissimilar? From now on, if you're ever told that a significant educational test has "high reliability," you are permitted to ask, ever so suavely, "What kind or what kinds of reliability are you talking about?" (Most often, you'll find that the test developers have computed some type of internal consistency reliability, because it's possible to calculate such reliability coefficients on the basis of only one test administration. Both of the other two kinds of reliability require at least two test administrations.) It's also important to note that reliability in one area does not ensure reliability in another. Don't assume, for example, that a test with high internal consistency reliability will automatically yield stable scores over time. It just isn't so.

Reliability in the Classroom

So, what sorts of reliability evidence should classroom teachers collect for their own tests? My answer may surprise you. I don't think teachers need to assemble *any kind* of reliability evidence. There's just too little payoff for the effort involved.

I do believe that classroom teachers ought to understand test reliability, especially that it comes in three quite distinctive forms and that one type of reliability definitely isn't equivalent to another. And this is the point at which even reliability has a relationship to instruction, although I must confess it's not a strong relationship. Suppose your students are taking important external tests—say, statewide achievement tests assessing their mastery of state-sanctioned content standards. Well, if the tests are truly important, why not find out something about their technical characteristics? Is there evidence of assessment reliability presented? If so, what kind or what kinds of reliability evidence?

If the statewide test's reliability evidence is skimpy, then you should be uneasy about the test's quality. Here's why: *An unreliable test will rarely yield scores from which valid inferences can be drawn.*

I'll illustrate this point with an example of stability evidence of reliability. Suppose your students took an important exam on Tuesday morning, and there was a fire in the school counselor's office on Tuesday afternoon. Your student's exam papers went up in smoke. A week later, you re-administer the big test, only to learn soon after that the original exam papers were saved from the flames by an intrepid school custodian. When you compare the two sets of scores on the very same exam administered a week apart, you are surprised to find that your students' scores seem to bounce all over the place. For example, Billy scored high on the first test, yet scored low on the second. Tristan scored low on the first test, but soared on the second.

Based on the variable test scores, have these students mastered the material or haven't they? Would it be appropriate or inappropriate to send Billy on to more challenging work? Does Tristan need extra guided practice, or is she ready for independent application? If a test is unreliable—inconsistent—how can it contribute to accurate score-based inferences and sound instructional decisions? Answer: It can't.

Assessment Bias

Bias is something that everyone understands to be a bad thing. Bias beclouds one's judgment. Conversely, the absence of bias is a good thing; it permits better judgment. *Assessment bias* is one species of bias and, as you might have already guessed, it's something educators need to identify and eliminate, both for moral reasons and in the interest of promoting better, more defensible instructional decisions. Let's see how to go about doing that for large-scale tests and for the tests that teachers cook up for their own students.

The Nature of Assessment Bias

Assessment bias occurs whenever test items offend or unfairly penalize students for reasons related to students' personal characteristics, such as their race, gender, ethnicity, religion, or socioeconomic status. Notice that there are two elements in this definition of assessment bias. A test can be biased if it *offends* students or if it *unfairly penalizes* students because of students' personal characteristics.

An example of a test item that would offend students might be one in which a person, clearly identifiable as a member of a particular ethnic group, is described in the item itself as displaying patently unintelligent behavior. Students from that same ethnic group might (with good reason) be upset at the test item's implication that persons of their ethnicity are not all that bright. And that sort of upset often leads the offended students to perform less well than would otherwise be the case. Another example of offensive test items would arise if females were always depicted in a test's items as being employed in low-level, undemanding jobs whereas males were always depicted as holding high-paying, executive positions. Girls taking a test composed of such sexist items might (again, quite properly) be annoyed and, hence, might perform less well than they would have otherwise.

Turning to unfair penalization, think about a series of mathematical items set in a context of how to score a football game. If girls participate less frequently in football and watch, in general, fewer football games on television, then girls are likely to have more diffi-culty in answering math items that revolve around how many points are awarded when a team "scores a safety" or "kicks extra points rather than running or passing for extra points." These sorts of math-ematics items simply shimmer with gender bias.

Not all penalties are unfair, of course. If students don't study properly and then perform poorly on a teacher's test, such penalties are richly deserved. What's more, the inference a teacher would make, based on these low scores, would be a valid one: These students haven't mastered the material! But if students' personal characteris-tics, such as their socioeconomic status (SES), are a determining fac-tor in weaker test performance, then assessment bias has clearly raised its unattractive head. It distorts the accuracy of students' test performances and invariably leads to invalid inferences about stu-dents' status and to unsound instructional decisions about how best to teach those students.

Bias Detection in Large-Scale Assessments

There was a time, not too long ago, when the creators of large-scale tests (such as nationally standardized achievement tests) didn't do a particularly respectable job of identifying and excising biased items from their tests. I taught educational measurement courses in the UCLA Graduate School of Education for many years, and in the late 1970s, one of the nationally standardized achievement tests I rou-tinely had my students critique employed a bias-detection procedure that would be considered laughable today. Even back then, it made me smirk a bit.

Here's how the test-developers' bias-detection procedure worked. A *three*-person bias review committee was asked to review all of the items of a test under development. Two of the reviewers "represented" minority groups. If *all three reviewers* considered an item to be biased, the item was eliminated from the test. Otherwise, that item stayed on the test. If the two minority-representing reviewers considered an item biased beyond belief, but the third reviewer disagreed, the item stayed. Today, such a superficial bias-review process would be recognized as absurd.

Developers of large-scale tests now employ far more rigorous bias-detection procedures, especially with respect to bias based on race and gender. A typical approach these days calls for the creation of a bias-review committee, usually of 15–25 members, almost all of whom are themselves members of minority groups. Bias-review committees are typically given ample training and practice in how best to render their item-bias judgments. For each item that might end up being included in the test, every member of the bias-review committee would be asked to respond to the following question:

Might this item offend or unfairly penalize students because of such personal characteristics as gender, ethnicity, religion, or socioeconomic status?

_____ Yes   _____ No   _____ Uncertain

Note that the above question asks reviewers to judge whether a student *might* be penalized, not whether the item *would* (for absolutely certain) penalize a student. This kind of phrasing makes it clear that the test's developers are going the extra mile to eliminate any items that *might possibly* offend or unfairly penalize students because of personal characteristics. If the review question asked whether an item "would" offend or unfairly penalize students, you can bet that fewer items would be reported as biased.

If a certain percentage of bias-reviewers believe the item might be biased, it is eliminated from those to be used in the test. Clearly, the determination of what proportion of reviewers is needed to delete an item on potential-bias grounds represents an important issue. With the three-person bias-review committee my 1970s students read about at UCLA, the percentage of reviewers necessary for an item's elimination was 100 percent. In recent years I have taken part in bias-review procedures where an item would eliminated if more than five percent of the reviewers rated the item as biased. Times have definitely changed.

My experiences suggest that the developers of most of our current large-scale tests have been attentive to the potential presence of assessment bias based on students' gender or membership in a minority racial or ethnic group. (I still think that today's major educational tests feature far too many items that are biased on SES grounds. We'll discuss this issue in Chapter 9.) There may be a few items that have slipped by the rigorous item-review process but, in general, those test developers get an *A* for effort. In many instances, such assiduous attention to gender and minority-group bias eradication stems directly from the fear that any adverse results of their tests might be challenged in court. The threat of litigation often proves to be a potent stimulant!

Assessment Bias in the Classroom

Unfortunately, there's much more bias present in teachers' classroom tests than most teachers imagine. The reason is not that today's classroom teachers deliberately set out to offend or unfairly penalize certain of their students; it's just that too few teachers have systematically attended to this issue.

The key to unbiasing tests is a simple matter of serious, item-by-item scrutiny. The same kind of item-review question that bias-reviewers typically use in their appraisal of large-scale assessments will work for classroom tests, too. A teacher who is instructing students from racial/ethnic groups other than the teacher's own racial/ethnic group might be wise to ask a colleague (or a parent) from those racial/ethnic groups to serve as a one-person bias review committee. This can be very illuminating. Happily, most biased items can be repaired with only modest effort. Those that can't should be tossed.

This whole bias-detection business is about being fair to all students and assessing them in such a way that they are accurately measured. That's the only way a teacher's test-based inferences will be valid. And, of course, valid inferences about students serve as the foundation for defensible instructional decisions. Invalid inferences don't.

INSTRUCTIONALLY FOCUSED TESTING TIPS

• Recognize that validity refers to a test-based inference, not to the test itself.

• Understand that there are three kinds of validity evidence, all of which can contribute to the confidence teachers have in the accuracy of a test-based inference about students.

• Assemble content-related evidence of validity for your most important classroom tests.

• Know that there are three related, but meaningfully different kinds of reliability evidence that can be collected for educational tests.

• Give serious attention to the detection and elimination of assessment bias in classroom tests.

Recommended Resources

American Educational Research Association. (1999). *Standards for educational and psychological testing.* Washington, DC: Author.

McNeil, L. M. (2000, June). Creating new inequalities: Contradictions of reform. *Phi Delta Kappan, 81*(10), 728–734.

Popham, W. J. (2000). *Modern educational measurement: Practical guidelines for educational leaders* (3rd ed.). Boston: Allyn & Bacon.

Popham, W. J. (Program Consultant). (2000). *Norm- and criterion-referenced testing: What assessment-literate educators should know* [Videotape]. Los Angeles: IOX Assessment Associates.

Popham, W. J. (Program Consultant). (2000). *Standardized achievement tests: How to tell what they measure* [Videotape]. Los Angeles: IOX Assessment Associates.

5

An Introduction
to Test Building

I T'S TIME TO DIG INTO TEST-CONSTRUCTION AND THE INNARDS OF THE ITEMS THAT actually make up educational tests. In this brief chapter, and the two chapters following it, I'll be dispensing a series of rules to follow if you wish to create a set of spectacular items for your own classroom tests. Don't forget that there are some solid references cited at the end of each chapter. If you want to dig deeper into the rules for test-development and item-construction, I encourage you to explore one or more of the listed resources. Prior to picking up your shovel for any diligent item-digging, though, I need to remind you of some preliminary considerations you'll need to attend to before you've constructed even a single item.

All About Inferences

Since the early pages of this book, you've been reading that teachers use tests in order to make inferences about their students' cognitive or affective status. And, once those score-based inferences have been made, the teacher then reaches instructional decisions based (at least in part) on those inferences. Educational assessment revolves around inference making.

Well, if that is true (and you've already read it so often in this book, you *must* know that it's true), then why not focus on your intended score-based inferences throughout all of your test-development efforts? If you do so, your tests are more likely to generate data that will support valid inferences, and you are more likely to make better instructional decisions.

But what does this inference-focused approach to test-construction look like in the real world? Well, it means that before you begin to even think about a test and what it might look like, you first isolate the instructional *decisions* that need to be made. What are you going to use this test for? Will you be looking at the results to see if students have mastered a given curricular aim? Will you be looking at the results to find out what your students' current geometric understandings are so that you can decide on the most suitable content for your upcoming geometry unit? Perhaps, as is often the case, you'll be testing your students merely to assign grades for a given unit of study or, perhaps, for an entire term.

Clearly, the purposes for classroom tests can vary substantially, and the decisions linked to those purposes will also vary. But all of these purposes will be better satisfied if subsequent decisions are based on more accurate score-based inferences about students' cognitive or affective status. This three-step process is represented graphically in Figure 5.1, where you can see that *prior to test-construction,* a teacher should strive to identify the decisions that will be riding on the yet-to-be-built test's results and what sorts of score-based inferences will best contribute to the teacher's pre-identified decisions.

If you keep these two considerations—decisions and contributing-inferences—constantly in mind, often these considerations will shape the nature of the test itself. For instance, if you're trying to decide what to address instructionally, based on students' entry capabilities, you'll need substantially fewer test items than you would need if you were trying to decide what students' end-of-course grades should be. If your goal is to make decisions regarding your own

5.1 | THREE STEPS IN CLASSROOM TEST BUILDING

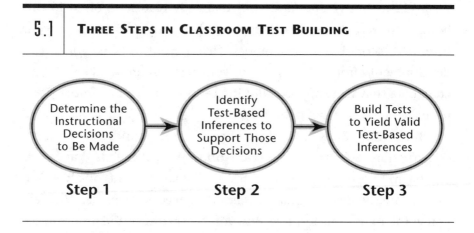

instructional effectiveness, you'll need more items still—enough to support reasonable inferences about what parts of your instructional program seemed to work and what parts didn't. The decision-at-issue, and the inferences that can best inform that decision, should always govern the particulars of a teacher's classroom assessments.

Don't forget that the most important kind of validity for classroom tests is content-related evidence of validity. Prior to test-building, a wonderful opportunity arises to make sure that the curricular aims to be assessed (the skills and knowledge to be taught) are satisfactorily represented in a classroom test. There should be no obvious content gaps, and the number and weighting of items on a test should be representative of the importance of the content standards being measured.

Almost all of these test-design decisions that a teacher makes are judgment calls. There are no sacrosanct 10 commandments of test construction, no inviolate rules about the numbers of needed items or the necessary breadth of content coverage. However, teachers who give serious attention to the preliminary questions reflected in Figure 5.1, namely, (1) the instructional decisions-at-issue and (2) the score-based inferences that best support those inferences, will be more likely to create a decent classroom test that helps improve their instruction.

Surely such teachers' tests will be meaningfully better than the class-room tests devised by teachers who immediately dive into item-development without first giving some thought to the upcoming decisions or inferences they'll need to make.

Two Item-Types

There are all sorts of tidy little distinctions in the field of educational measurement. We've talked about the differences between an apti-tude test and an achievement test. We have considered three varieties of validity evidence as well as three types of reliability. Assessment folks, it seems, love to conjure up categories into which measurement commodities can be tossed. The following two chapters are, in fact, based on another of those category schemes: a two-way division between the kinds of items that make up all educational tests.

Every item that nestles in an educational test can be classified either as a *selected-response* item or as a *constructed-response* item. The labels for these two item-categories do a pretty decent job of describ-ing the key feature of the items contained in each category. A *selected-response* item calls for students to select an answer from a set of pre-sented options. Multiple-choice items are usually the first sort of selected-response item that comes to most folks' minds. But True-False items are also members of the selected-response family because the test-taker must choose, that is, select, between two presented options, namely, True or False.

In contrast, a *constructed-response* item requires test-takers to respond by constructing, that is, *generating,* an answer, an essay, or whatever the item calls for. The most common kinds of constructed-response items are essay items and short-answer items. In each of those instances, the student must create a response, not merely choose a response from a set of already provided alternatives.

There are few teachers who haven't heard the usual critiques of selected-response and constructed-response items. It is often said that selected-response items, while easy to score, usually deal with low-level, readily memorizable content. Just as often it is said that constructed-response items, while eliciting higher-level cognitive responses from students, take far more time to score and are difficult to score with adequate objectivity. Like most things in life, there are clear trade-offs involved in the construction of classroom tests when choosing between selected-response and constructed-response items.

There is simply no body of assembled research indicating that one of these item-types is superior to the other. Clearly, it all depends. It depends on the curricular aims being measured. It depends on how much energy and time a teacher has available to score students' responses to constructed-response items. It depends on how skillful the teacher is in devising different sorts of test items. Generally speaking, teachers must first look carefully at the curricular aims to be sought, then try to develop tests—either selected-response or constructed-response—that seem most likely to yield valid score-based inferences about their students.

Irrespective of whether you end up favoring selected-response items, constructed-response items, or a hybrid mix of each, there are some experience-based guidelines that will help you dodge the most vile of the test-development shortcomings classroom teachers are apt to encounter.

Roadblocks to Good Item-Writing

In Chapter 6, I'll be considering item-construction rules for selected-response tests. In Chapter 7, I'll deal with rules for constructing and scoring students' performances on constructed-response tests. But first, I want share five obstacles to good item-writing that apply to *both* selected-response items and constructed-response items. These five roadblocks interfere with the purpose of test-items: to permit accurate inferences about students' status. They are (1) *unclear directions,* (2) *ambiguous statements,* (3) *unintentional clues,* (4) *complex phrasing,* and (5) *difficult vocabulary.* Let's run through each of these five obstacles. I'll supply an example of each of these roadblocks. Your job as a test-developer is to dodge all five obstacles. Such dodging can often be difficult.

Unclear Directions. You'd be surprised how often students fail to perform well on a classroom test simply because they don't really know what they're supposed to do. The sorts of shoddy direction-giving that students often encounter in the tests they take are illustrated in the following directions for a classroom midterm exam. These directions may be fictitious, but they are strikingly similar to the kinds of directions most students see week in and week out.

DREADFUL DIRECTIONS

Directions: This midterm exam consists of four parts. Each part contains different types of items, for example, short-answer and multiple-choice items. Each of the exam's four parts covers one of the major units you have studied thus far during the course. Work your way through the items efficiently because there is a *time limit* for exam-completion. Do your best. Good luck!

These fictitious directions are, indeed, dreadful because they give students no guidance about the weighting of the exam's four parts. Because some of the four parts contain both selected-response items and constructed-response items, it certainly is possible that the teacher might regard particular parts of the exam as more important than other parts of the exam. Nonetheless, these directions don't give students a clue about differential weighting.

Notice, too, that the directions allude to a need for efficiency because of the *italicized* "time limit." What is that time limit? Should students devote equal time to the four parts which, based on these dismal directions, might contain equal or different numbers of items? Given these illustrative directions, students simply don't know the answers to a number of important issues that they will surely face during the exam.

As the creator of your own classroom tests, you will typically have a very thorough understanding of how you're expecting your students to respond. Remember, though, that *most* of your students cannot read your mind. (Fear those who can!) To make sure the directions to your tests are clear and complete, try to put yourself "inside the head" of one of your students, perhaps a less-swift student, and then silently read your test's directions from that student's perspective. If what a test-taker is supposed to do appears to be even slightly opaque, then spruce up your directions until their meaning is unmistakable.

Ambiguous Statements. Unless you are a diplomat, ambiguity is something to be avoided. It's especially reprehensible in educational tests, where it can be found in hazy directions (as in the preceding item-writing roadblock) and, even more critically, in the items themselves. Again, ambiguous statements usually appear because teachers "know what they mean" when they write an item. Students, unfortunately, are not in on that secret.

Consider the following ambiguous True-False item:

An Ambiguity-Laden True-False Item

T F   Several research studies show that adults often
        become domineering toward young children
        because of their inherited characteristics.

Does the "their" in this item refer to characteristics inherited by the domineering adults or to the characteristics inherited by the young children?

This is actually an easy item to fix. All the teacher needs to do is replace the ambiguity-inducing pronoun with the name of the group to which it refers. Faulty-reference pronouns are a common cause of ambiguity, as are words or phrases that might have double meanings in the context of the item.

Unintentional Clues. Sometimes teachers accidentally include clues that help less knowledgeable students appear more knowledgeable. A frequent example in multiple-choice tests is when teachers' consistently make the correct answer-option longer than the other answer-options. Typically, the extra length results from teachers' incorporating qualifiers to ensure that the correct answer is absolutely correct. Whatever the reason, if you routinely make your correct answers longer than your incorrect answers, all but your truly clucko students will figure out what's going on.

Another fairly common flaw in teacher-written multiple-choice items occurs when there is a grammatical tip-off regarding which answer-option is the winning answer-option. Consider the following example dealing with biological terminology and you'll see what I mean.

A GRAMMATICALLY CLUED GIVE-AWAY ITEM

The commonly recognized example of a **pachyderm** is an
 a. elephant.
 b. turtle.
 c. lion.
 d. pigeon.

Yes, the use of the article "an" in the first part of the item makes it clear that the first letter of the correct answer needs to be a vowel. And because "elephant" is the only answer-choice that fills the bill, it is embarrassingly obvious that choice *a* is the correct answer. An easy way to fix such an item would have been to put all the needed articles in the answer choices so that those choices would be (a) an elephant, (b) a turtle, (c) a lion, and (d) a pigeon.

Another common instance of unintentional clue dispensing occurs when teachers toss a "never" or "always" into the false statements of True-False items. Most students will recognize that there are few absolutes in life, so it's prudent to choose a "false" response for any items containing "never," "always," or "absolutely."

Inadvertent clues muck up the accuracy of score-based inferences by making it appear that some students have mastered a given curricular aim when, in reality, they haven't. The more inadvertent clues that you allow to creep into your classroom tests, the more "false positives" you will have on your hands. As before, prior to administering a test, review all items carefully to see if there are any aspects of an item that tip off the correct response.

Complex Phrasing. There are ways to say things simply, and there are ways to say things opaquely. In item-writing, simplicity wins and opacity loses. Beware of lengthy sentences in your items—sentences that begin to resemble a novella. Also, if your items contain so many *whos* or *whiches* that most sentences require a pronoun-eradicator, then *simplify.* We don't want students coming up with incorrect responses because they couldn't untangle an item's complicated construction.

See the snarled syntax in the following illustrative history item:

A CONSUMMATELY COMPLEX RIGHT-WRONG ITEM

Right or Wrong: Having been established following World War II in a patent ploy to accomplish that which the League of Nations failed to carry out subsequent to World War I, namely, peace-preservation, the United Nations (headquartered in New York) has, on a number of occasions, taken part in armed peacekeeping interventions throughout various parts of the world.

There is probably a core idea nestled somewhere in this comma-laden catastrophe of a sentence, but it is truly tough to figure out what that core idea is. How can students determine if such a meandering statement is right or wrong when they can't detect what the statement is really saying? When you churn out your test items, strive for simplicity.

Difficult Vocabulary. Test items are not the place for teachers to display their verbal sophistication or boost their self-esteem through the use of high-toned words. Skilled writers will always pitch their vocabulary at a level apt to be understood by their readers. Remember, the readers of your tests will be students—students whose vocabularies probably don't match your own. Therefore, eschew polysyllabic verbiage in your items. In fact, eschew phrases such as "eschew polysyllabic verbiage."

Here's an example of a high-school language arts item (10th grade literature) with a vocabulary level that's altogether too high:

A POLYSYLLABICALLY INUNDATED MULTIPLE-CHOICE ITEM

Considering the quintessential phenomenological attribute evinced by Mrs. Watkins in the short story you just read, which of the following options best characterizes that attribute?
- a. superabundant garrulousness
- b. a paucity of profundity
- c. hyperbolic affectations
- d. mellifluous articulation

If this teacher wants students to be able to discern what makes the fictional Mrs. Watkins tick, why not ask them in language that normal folks can comprehend?

Wrap Up

Looking back at this brief introduction to building your own classroom tests, you'll hopefully recall that the central mission of all such assessment is (1) to help you make valid inferences about your students so you can then (2) make better decisions about how to instruct those students. Never, *never* create a test just to be creating a test.

Always focus on the instructional decisions that are at issue and, based on those decisions, try to isolate the sorts of inferences about students you'll need to arrive at in order to make those decisions more defensibly. Beyond the mission of making inferences about your students based on their test performances, there is no other reason to test those students.

I have also indicated that when it comes time to put together your own classroom tests, the items you'll be using are always going to be, by definition, either selected-response items, constructed-response items, or a combination of those two item-types. There are advantages and disadvantages of both item-types.

Finally, I offered one hopefully useful test-construction suggestion. For *every* test that you create, review all items and directions from the perspective of your students. When you reconsider your items "using students' eyes," you'll almost always be able to improve your tests. And by "improve" them, I mean make them better instruments for uncovering students' covert cognitive and affective status.

INSTRUCTIONALLY FOCUSED TESTING TIPS

- Do not commence any test-construction activity until you have isolated, with genuine clarity, (1) the instructional decisions-at-issue and (2) the score-based inferences that will best support those decisions.

- Judiciously employ selected-response items and constructed-response items so that your test-based inferences are likely to be valid.

- Avoid the five roadblocks to good item-writing: unclear directions, ambiguous statements, unintentional clues, complex phrasing, and difficult vocabulary.

Recommended Resources

Linn, R. L., & Gronlund, N. E. (2000). *Measurement and assessment in teaching* (8th ed.). Upper Saddle River, NJ: Merrill.

McMillan, J. H. (2001). *Classroom assessment: Principles and practice for effective instruction* (2nd ed.). Boston: Allyn & Bacon.

Northwest Regional Educational Laboratory. (1991). *Paper-and-pencil test development* [Videotape]. Los Angeles: IOX Assessment Associates.

Stiggins, R. J. (Program Consultant). (1996). *Assessing reasoning in the classroom: A professional development video* [Videotape]. Portland, OR: Assessment Training Institute.

Stiggins, R. J. (2001). *Student-involved classroom assessment* (4th ed.). Upper Saddle River, NJ: Prentice Hall.

Selected-Response Items

In this chapter, I'll be describing selected-response items, focusing on the three main types: (1) *binary-choice items,* (2) *matching items,* and (3) *multiple-choice items.* I'll first take a quick peek at the advantages and disadvantages of each item-type and then list a set of rules for constructing that kind of item.

Binary-Choice Items

A *binary-choice item* is one in which the test-taker must choose between only two options. The most common kind of binary-choice item is the True-False item, in which students are given a set of statements and then asked to indicate whether each statement is true or false.

Perhaps you've never encountered the phrase "binary-choice" before, and you suspect I'm trying to impress you by tossing out an esoteric assessment term. What I want you to realize is that you can build all sorts of decent test items by presenting students with a two-choice challenge. The student's choices, for instance, could be between *right* and *wrong, correct* and *incorrect, accurate* or *inaccurate,* and so on. If you think of binary-choice items only as True-False, you may overlook some useful dichotomous-item possibilities.

Incidentally, there's a lesser known variation on this selected-response item-type that I've found very useful over the years. It's called a *multiple binary-choice item*. Here's how it works. First, the student is given a somewhat lengthy stimulus passage of perhaps two or three paragraphs. Then, after reading the paragraphs, the student must respond to *each* item in a set of four to six binary-choice items based directly on those paragraphs. When I taught educational measurement classes at UCLA, my midterm exams consisted of 50 items. I used 10 multiparagraph descriptions of measurement-related events, each of which was followed by 5 binary-choice items based on the description. My final exam was twice that long: 20 sets of stimulus material and 100 binary-choice items. I always thought my tests were terrific. That benign view, of course, may merely represent another form of assessment bias!

Seriously, though, if you asked any of my former students about my midterm or final exams, they'd tell you that the multiple binary-choice items I used were *tough*. Binary-choice items are not necessarily "easy," a lazy way out, or focused on low-level cognitive challenges. My tests included all sorts of challenges. My students had to consider previously unencountered stimulus information (in two or three paragraphs) and then make subtle decisions for each of the related binary-choice items. Remember, even with two options, it is possible to present students with a pair of choices that require a sophisticated understanding to sort out.

Advantages and Disadvantages

The chief advantage of binary-choice items is their terseness, which allows a teacher to cover a wide range of content by using a swarm of such items. For instance, if a history teacher wanted to discover if students knew a ton of facts about U.S. history, then a collection of Right-Wrong or True-False items would be an efficient way to uncover students' knowledge of those facts.

The major disadvantage of binary-choice items is that when they are used exclusively, they tend to promote memorization of factual information: names, dates, definitions, and so on. While factual information is often a necessary component of instruction, few would hold it up as the sole objective. Yes, it is possible for teachers to build subtleties into their binary-choice items, but teachers are often tempted to write out a statement that is quite decisively either true or false. Some teachers simply lift statements from textbooks, then toss a "not" (or, if in a foul mood, two "nots") into some of those statements. From a student's perspective, of course, the best way to prepare for those sorts of fact-based items is to memorize, memorize, memorize.

Some argue that another weakness of binary-choice items is that students can "guess their way to success." On probabilistic grounds, for each binary-choice item, an unadulterated guess is apt to be correct 50 percent of the time. Well, that's true for a *single* binary-choice item, but when students must cope with 10 or 20 such items, raw guesswork just won't work. A student would need to be extremely lucky to guess to success on a 20-item binary-choice test. Odds are that a student would stumble onto the correct answers for only about 10 of the 20 items . . . and 50 percent correct on a binary-choice test should not evoke applause *or* lead a teacher to infer that the student had mastered the material.

Summing up, binary-choice items can cover considerable content, but their use may encourage students to engage in massive memorization rather than try to acquire any sort of higher-level intellectual mastery of a body of content.

Item-Writing Rules

To keep your reading requirements from becoming onerous, I'm going to dispense all of this book's item-writing rules in a short-order manner. Each rule I present will be followed by few sentences to clarify or qualify the rule. And often, but not always, I'll toss in an example of a test item that is either consistent with the rule or violates that rule. I hope these illustrative test items will help you see how the item-writing rules should be followed. As is always the case, the rules are intended to help you, the teacher, arrive at more accurate inferences about what's going on inside your students' heads.

▲ **Generate binary-choice items in pairs, not singly.** Because binary-choice items work best when they are sampling two discrete categories (e.g., true or false), if there is a statement representing one of those categories, there ought to be an opposite statement representing the other category. It's a time-saving tactic to create both items at once, and if you can't, then you probably don't have even one good binary-choice item. Putting it another way, because your binary choices need to be mutually exclusive, there really ought to be readily reversible statements lurking out there. You might use only one item in a given test, but then you will have a nifty unused item for next year!

▲ **Phrase each item so that a cursory reading leads to an incorrect answer.** Knowing that binary-choice items may encourage students to memorize, it's the teacher's responsibility to do everything possible to ensure that memorization is accurate. If you routinely word binary-choice items so that a superficial reading will lead students toward wrong answers, then students will soon learn to read those items with care. Take a look at the following example:

PHRASING THAT FOILS A SUPERFICIAL RESPONSE

T   F   Given that almost all teachers care deeply about
              the progress of their students, and recognizing the
              inherent diversity in the cognitive capabilities of
              those students, most classroom teachers design
              truly individualized instructional programs for their
              students. (Answer: False)

Notice that although the item-writer uses appealing phrases ("care deeply" and "inherent diversity in the cognitive capabilities") that might incline a casual or lazy reader toward a validating "True" response, closer analysis would reveal that the practical realities of classrooms preclude "most" teachers from designing "truly individualized" programs. This rule is not about trying to trick students into making mistakes; rather, it's a reminder to develop your students' disposition to read all binary-choice items carefully and respond thoughtfully.

▲ **Avoid negative statements, and never use double negatives.** In Right-Wrong or True-False items, negatively phrased statements make it needlessly difficult for students to decide whether that statement is accurate or inaccurate. Consider the following perplexingly stated item:

TOO-NUMEROUS NEGATIVES

T F   It is hardly ever the case that students' lack of interest in a subject such as science will disincline teachers to give those students very low grades. (Answer: Who knows?)

When you create binary-choice items, be sure to steer clear of negativity, especially doubly confusing, doubled-up negativity.

▲ **Restrict single-item statements to single concepts.** If you double-up two concepts in a single item statement, how does a student respond if one concept is accurate and the other isn't? Take a look at this confusing item:

A DOUBLE-CONCEPT TRUE-FALSE ITEM

T F   Today's professional tennis players serve the ball at much faster speeds than yesteryear's players because of high-tech racquets. (Answer: Sort of True)

Yes, there are two separate concepts in this single statement: the incidence of faster tennis serves and the *reason* for those faster serves. One or both may be true.

▲ **Use an approximately equal number of items, reflecting the two categories tested.** There is no need for a 20-item Right-Wrong test to have precisely 10 *right* items and 10 *wrong* items. Still, avoid having one of your two categories represented by 80 or 90 percent of your statements. If you typically overbook on *false* items in your True-False tests, students who are totally at sea about an item will be apt to opt for a *false* answer and will probably be correct.

▲ **Make statements representing both binary categories equal in length.** Again, to avoid giving away the correct answers, don't make all your *false* statements brief and (in an effort to include necessary qualifiers) make all your *true* statements long. Students catch on quickly to this kind of test-making tendency.

Matching Items

A *matching item* consists of two lists of words or phrases. The test-taker must match components in one list (the *premises,* typically presented on the left) with components in the other list (the *responses,* typically presented on the right), according to a particular kind of association indicated in the item's directions. Here's an illustrative matching item based on my favorite films.

A MATCHING ITEM

Directions. On the line to the left of each film category in Column A, write the letter of the film from Jim's Favorite Films in Column B that represents that type of film. Each film in Column B may be used no more than once.

Column A: Film Categories	Column B: Jim's Favorite Films
____ 1. Action Adventure	a. *The American President*
____ 2. Western	b. *Gunga Din*
____ 3. Musical	c. *Mrs. Miniver*
____ 4. Romance	d. *Red River*
	e. *The Sound of Music*

(Answers: 1: b, 2: d, 3: e, 4: a)

Advantages and Disadvantages

Like binary-choice items, matching items can cover a good deal of territory in an efficient fashion, and they are a great choice if you're interesting in finding out if your students have memorized factual information. (Of course, memorization is a lower-level goal.) Matching items sometimes can work well if you want your students to cross-reference and integrate their knowledge regarding the listed premises and responses. However, because matching items require pools of related ideas, such items don't work well if you're trying to assess your students' mastery of distinctive ideas.

Item-Writing Rules

Most of the rules for constructing matching items are fairly self-explanatory.

▲ **Use fairly brief lists, placing the shorter entries on the right.** If the premises and responses in a matching item are too long, students tend to lose track of what they originally set out to look for. The words and phrases that make up the premises should be short, and those that make up the responses should be shorter still.

▲ **Employ homogeneous lists.** Both the list of premises and responses must be composed of similar sorts of things. If not, an alert student will be able to come up with the correct associations simply by "elimination" because some entries in the premises or responses stand out too much from their siblings. For instances, if I had included *Kung Fu Halloween III* as a possible response for my favorite-film matching item, I have little doubt that you would have discarded it immediately.

▲ **Include more responses than premises.** If you use the exact same number of responses as premises in a matching item, then a student who knows half or more of the correct associations is in position to guess the rest of the associations with pretty decent odds. Make it tougher to get lucky by tossing in at least a few extra responses.

▲ **List responses in a logical order.** This rule is designed to make sure you don't accidentally give away hints about which responses hook up with which premises. Choose a logical ordering scheme for your responses (say, alphabetical or chronological) and stick with it. In my Favorite Films example, I listed the responses alphabetically.

▲ **Describe the basis for matching and the number of times a response can be used.** To satisfy this rule, you need to make sure your test's directions clarify the nature of the associations you want students to use when they identify matches. Regarding the student's use of responses, a phrase such as the following is often employed: "Each response in the list at the right may be used once, more than once, or not at all."

▲ **Try to place all premises and responses for any matching item on a single page.** This rule's intent is to spare your students lots of potentially confusing flipping back and forth in order to accurately link responses to premises. During exams, it also makes for a quieter classroom.

Multiple-Choice Items

The most popular type of selected-response item has got to be the *multiple-choice item*. A student is first given either a question or a partially complete statement. This part of the item is referred to as the item's *stem*. Then three or more potential answer-options are presented. These are usually called *alternatives* or *options*.

Multiple-choice items are widely employed, especially for large-scale assessments, because the format allows students' responses to be electronically scanned. More recently, modestly priced scanners are increasingly available to teachers for use in scoring their students' responses to teacher-made, or commercially distributed, multiple-choice tests.

There are two important variants in a multiple-choice item: (1) whether the stem consists of a *direct question* or an *incomplete statement* and (2) whether the student's choice of alternatives is supposed to be a *correct answer* or a *best answer*. I've worked the four variations into the following two sample items.

A Direct-Question (Best-Answer) Multiple-Choice Item

During the early years of this century, which of the following states has experienced the most difficulties in supplying its citizens with electrical power?

    a. California

    b. Kansas

    c. Louisiana

    d. Washington

An Incomplete-Statement (Correct-Answer) Multiple-Choice Item

The capital of Oregon is

    a. Columbia.

    b. Portland.

    c. Salem.

    d. Sacramento.

Although there are some exceptions, direct questions usually make for better multiple-choice questions than incomplete statements do, simply because there's less chance for confusion. This is especially true for children in the early grades, who don't have tons of experience making sense out of incomplete statements. And, generally speaking, best-answer items *work* better than correct-answer items because the format allows item-writers to build gradients of correctness into the alternatives and, thereby, increase the challenge. To illustrate, the response to the Best Answer example question ought to be choice *a* (California). A test-taker might be inclined to choose one of the other three states listed (Washington, because of its hydroelectric power; Louisiana, because of its petroleum reserves; or Kansas, because it lacks either of these resources). However, the *best* answer at this particular time in the 21st century is demonstrably "California."

Advantages and Disadvantages

A key plus of the multiple-choice item is its widespread applicability to the assessment of cognitive skills and knowledge, as well as to the measurement of students' affect. (See Chapter 8.) It really is a remarkably versatile format. Another advantage of multiple-choice items is that it's possible to make them quite varied in the levels of difficulty they possess. Cleverly constructed multiple-choice items can present very high-level cognitive challenges to students. (In graduate school, the most difficult test items I encountered were the carefully crafted multiple-choice items in a philosophy of education course. The distinctions among answer options were incredibly subtle.) And, of course, as with all selected-response items, multiple-choice items are fairly easy to score. Finally, and this is a big plus from an instructional perspective, the multiple-choice format allows teachers to build in certain wrong-answer alternatives that, if chosen by many students, will signal the need to deal with particular types of students' misunderstandings.

The key weakness of multiple-choice items is that when students review a set of alternatives for an item, they may be able to recognize a correct answer that they would never have been able to generate on their own. In that sense, multiple-choice items can present an exaggerated picture of a student's understanding or competence, which might lead teachers to invalid inferences.

Another serious weakness, one shared by all selected-response items, is that multiple-choice items can never measure a student's ability to creatively synthesize content of any sort. Finally, in an effort to come up with the necessary number of plausible alternatives, novice item-writers sometimes toss in some alternatives that are blatantly incorrect. This shortcoming, of course, is more a weakness of the item-writer than the item-type. Like all test items, a multiple-choice item's value as a tool for ferreting out educational variables is predicated on the item-writer's skill; however, multiple-items do seem to be less forgiving. If you're trying to create a four-alternative multiple-choice item and two or more of your alternatives are giveaways, then you're numerically back to a binary-choice item . . . or a dead giveaway. Note the patent absurdity of three of the alternatives in the following mouse-related item:

DISMAL DISTRACTERS

What are the names of Mickey Mouse's two nephews?
    a. Huey, Dewey, and Louie
    b. Louie Dewey
    c. Morty and Ferdy
    d. Minnie

Item-Writing Rules

Well-constructed multiple-choice items, when deployed along with other types of items, can make a genuine contribution to a teacher's assessment arsenal. Here are some useful rules for you to follow.

▲ **The question or problem in the stem must be self-contained.** Sometimes, beginning item-writers fail to make a multiple-choice item's stem sufficiently complete so that a student can read the stem and then set out to select the best (or correct) answer from the alternatives. The stem should contain as much of the item's content as possible, thereby rendering the alternatives much shorter than would otherwise be the case.

▲ **Avoid negatively stated stems.** Just as with binary-choice items, negatively stated stems can engender genuine confusion in students.

▲ **Each alternative must be grammatically consistent with the item's stem.** Think back to the item-writing roadblocks presented in Chapter 5, one of which was to give students no unintended clues. Well, as you can see from the next sample item, grammatical inconsistency for three of these answer-options supplies students with a whopping unintended clue.

A NON-SHERLOCKIAN CLUE

In our federal government, the individuals who exercise ultimate authority over legislation and executive actions are the

    a. president.

    b. vice president.

    c. Speaker of the House of Representatives.

    d. justices of the Supreme Court.

▲ **Make all alternatives plausible, but be sure that one of them is indisputably the correct or best answer.** As I indicated when describing the weaknesses of multiple-choice items, teachers sometimes toss in one or more implausible alternatives, thereby diminishing the item substantially. Although avoiding that problem is important, it's even more important to make certain that you really do have one *bona fide* correct answer in any item's list of alternatives, rather than two similar answers, either of which could be arguably correct.

▲ **Randomly use all answer positions in approximately equal numbers.** Too many teachers, reluctant to "give away" the correct answer too early, tend to concentrate correct answers in the *C*, *D*, or *E* range of alternatives. It doesn't take students long to figure out this kind of pattern. If you use four-option items, make sure that roughly one-fourth of the correct answers turn out to be *A*, one-fourth *B*, and so on.

▲ **Never use "all of the above" as an answer choice, but use "none of the above" to make items more demanding.** Students often become confused when confronted with items that have more than one correct answer. Usually, what happens is they'll see one correct alternative and instantly opt for it without recognizing that there are other correct options later in the list. Although using "all of the above" is always improper, tests involving content such as mathematics can be made more difficult by presenting three or four answer options, none of which is correct, followed by a correct "none-of-the-above" option.

Selected-Response Items and Instruction

By this point in the book, I know you know that the reason teachers test their students is to get a fix on students' status with respect to covert educational variables. Rarely will one kind of selected-response test item do such a thorough job that a teacher can come up with a valid inference about the student's status based on that one item-type alone. Accordingly, I recommend that you operationalize your curricular targets by using different types of items. Remember, to get your students ready to display their mastery in myriad ways, you must use your instruction to promote a level of *generalizable mastery*, the kind that can display itself via students' responses to various types of test items, both selected-response *and* constructed-response. More importantly, when your students leave you, they will be able to use their generalizably mastered skills and knowledge throughout the remainder of their schooling and throughout the rest of their lives.

INSTRUCTIONALLY FOCUSED TESTING TIPS

• Become familiar with the advantages and disadvantages of binary-choice, matching, and multiple-choice items.

• If you use these types of selected-response items in your classroom tests, make certain to follow experience-based rules for creating each item type.

Recommended Resources

Haladyna, T. M. (1999). *Developing and validating multiple-choice test items* (2nd ed.). Mahwah, NJ: Lawrence Erlbaum Associates.

Linn, R. L., & Gronlund, N. E. (2000). *Measurement and assessment in teaching* (8th ed.). Upper Saddle River, NJ: Merrill.

McMillan, J. H. (2001). *Classroom assessment: Principles and practice for effective instruction* (2nd ed.). Boston: Allyn & Bacon.

Northwest Regional Educational Laboratory. (1991). *Paper-and-pencil test development* [Videotape]. Los Angeles: IOX Assessment Associates.

Popham, W. J. (Program Consultant). (1996). *Creating challenging classroom tests: When students SELECT their answers* [Videotape]. Los Angeles: IOX Assessment Associates.

Popham, W. J. (2002). *Classroom assessment: What teachers need to know* (3rd ed.). Boston: Allyn & Bacon.

Stiggins, R. J. (Program Consultant). (1996). *Common sense paper and pencil assessments: A professional development video* [Videotape]. Portland, OR: Assessment Training Institute.

Constructed-Response Items

IN THIS CHAPTER, I'LL BE DESCRIBING THE TWO MOST COMMON TYPES OF constructed-response items: *short-answer* items and *essay* items. Just as in the previous chapter, I'll briefly discuss the advantages and disadvantages of these two item-types and then provide a concise set of item-construction rules for each. From there, I'll address how to evaluate students' responses to essay items or, for that matter, to any type of constructed-response item. We'll take a good look at how *rubrics* are employed—not only to evaluate students' responses, but also to teach students how they *should* respond. Finally, we'll consider *performance assessment* and *portfolio assessment*, two currently popular but fairly atypical forms of constructed-response testing.

Constructed-Response Assessment: Positives and Negatives

The chief virtue of any type of constructed-response item is that it requires students to create their responses rather than select a prepackaged response from the answer shelf. Clearly, creating a response represents a more complicated and difficult task. Some students who might stumble onto a selected-response item's correct answer simply by casting a covetous eye over the available options would never be able to concoct an original correct answer without access to such options. Constructed-response items, in a word, are *tougher* for test-takers. And, because a student really needs to understand something in order to construct a response based on that understanding, in many instances (but not all), students' responses to these sorts of items will better contribute to valid inferences than will students' answers to selected-response items.

On the downside, students' answers to constructed-response items take longer to score, and it's also more of challenge to score them accurately. In fact, the more complex the task that's presented to students in a constructed-response item, the tougher it is for teachers to score. Whereas a teacher might have little difficulty accurately scoring a student's one-word response to a short-answer item, a 1,000-word essay is another matter entirely. The teacher might score the long essay too leniently or too strictly. And if asked to evaluate the same essay a month later, it's very possible that the teacher might give the essay a very different score.

As a side note, a decade or so ago, some states created elaborate large-scale tests that incorporated lots of constructed-response items; those states quickly learned how expensive it was to get those tests scored. That's because scoring constructed responses involves lots of human beings, not just electrically powered machines. Due to such substantial costs, most large-scale tests these days rely primarily on selected-response items. In most of those tests, however, you will still find a limited number of constructed-response items.

Clearly, there are pluses and minuses associated with the use of constructed-response items. As a teacher, however, *you* can decide whether *you* want to have your own tests include many, some, or no constructed-response items. Yes, the scoring of constructed-response items requires a greater time investment on your part. Still, I hope to convince you that constructed-response items will help you arrive at more valid inferences about your students' actual levels of mastery. What you'll soon see, when we consider *rubrics* later in the chapter, is that it's possible to conceptualize constructed-response items and the scoring for those items so that both you and your students will reap *giant* instructional payoffs. If you want your students to master truly powerful cognitive skills, you almost always need to rely on at least a certain number of constructed-response items.

Let's turn now to a closer inspection of the two most popular forms of constructed-response items: *short-answer items* and *essay items*.

Short-Answer Items

A short-answer item requires a student to supply a word, a phrase, or a sentence or two in response either to a direct question or an incomplete statement. A short-answer item's only real distinction from an essay item is in the brevity of the response the student is supposed to supply.

Advantages and Disadvantages

One virtue of short-answer items is that, like all constructed-response items, they require students to *generate* a response rather than plucking one from a set of already-presented options. The students' own words can offer a good deal of insight into their understanding, revealing if they are on the mark or conceptualizing something very differently from how the teacher intended it to be understood. Short-answer items have the additional advantage of being time-efficient; students can answer them relatively quickly, and teachers can score students' answers relatively easily. Thus, as is true with binary-choice and matching items, short-answer items allow test-making teachers to measure a substantial amount of content. A middle school social studies teacher interested in finding out whether students knew the meanings of a set of 25 technical terms could present a term's definition as the stimulus in each short-answer item, and then ask students to supply the name of the defined term. (Alternately, that teacher could present the names of terms and then ask for their full-blown definitions, but then the students' responses would be substantially longer than "short"!)

An item asking for a full definition, of course, would still be regarded as a short-answer item. The longer the short answer that's called for, the more class time the test will take up. However, the more revealing the responses may be. The single-word response, 25-item vocabulary test might take up 10 minutes of class time; the full-definition version of all 25 words might take about 30 minutes. But operationalizing a student's vocabulary knowledge in the form of a full-definition test would probably promote deeper understanding of the vocabulary terms involved. Shorter short-answer items, therefore, maximize the content-coverage value of this item-type, but also contribute to the item-type's disadvantages.

One of these disadvantages is that short-answer items tend to foster the student's memorization of factual information, which is another feature they have in common with binary-choice items. Teachers must be wary of employing many assessment approaches that fail to nudge students a bit higher on the cognitive ladder. Be sure to balance your assessment approaches and remember that gains in time and content coverage can also lead to losses in cognitive challenge.

In addition, although short-answer items are easier to score than essay items, they are still more difficult to score accurately than are selected-response items. Suppose, for example, that one student's response uses a similar but different word or phrase than the one the teacher was looking for. If the student's response is not identical to the teacher's "preferred" short answer, is the student right or wrong? And what about spelling? If a student's written response to "Who, in 1492, first set foot on America?" is "Column-bus," is this right or wrong? As you see, even in their most elemental form, constructed-response items can present teachers with some nontrivial scoring puzzles.

Item-Writing Rules

Again, my item-writing rules are ultra-short. If you wish to dig deeper into the nuances of creating good short-answer items, be sure to consult this chapter's recommended resources section.

▲ **Choose direct questions over incomplete statements.** There's less chance of confusing students, especially the little ones in grades K–3, if you write your short-answer items as direct questions rather than as incomplete statements. You'd be surprised how many times a teacher has one answer in mind for an incomplete statement, but ambiguities in that incomplete statement lead students to come up with answers that are dramatically different.

▲ **Structure an item so that it seeks a brief, unique response.** There's really a fair amount of verbal artistry associated with the construction of short-answer items, for the item should elicit a truly distinctive response that is also quite terse. I have a pair of examples for you to consider. Whereas the first item might elicit a considerable variety of responses from students, the second is far more likely to elicit the term that the teacher had in mind.

AN EXCESSIVELY OPEN CONSTRUCTION

What one word can be used to represent a general truth or
principle?
(Answer: Maxim . . . or truism? Aphorism? Axiom? Adage?)

A CHARMINGLY CONSTRAINED CONSTRUCTION,
OPAQUELY PHRASED

What one word describes an expression of a general truth
or principle, especially an aphoristic or sententious one?
(Answer: Maxim)

Incidentally, please observe that the second item, despite its worthy incorporation of constraints, flat-out violates Chapter 5's general item-writing roadblock concerning difficult vocabulary. When was the last time you used or heard anyone use the words "sententious" or "aphoristic"? By following one rule, item-writers sometimes risk breaking another. The trick, of course, is to figure out how to violate no rules at all. Occasionally, this is almost impossible. We may not live in a sin-free world, but we can at least strive to sin in moderation. Similarly, try to break as few item-writing rules as you can.

▲ **Place response-blanks at the end of incomplete statements or, for direct questions, in the margins.** If any of your short-answer items are based on incomplete statements, try to place your response-blanks near the end of the sentence. Early-on blanks tend to confuse students. For direct questions, the virtue of placing response-blanks in the margins is that it allows you to score the students' answers more efficiently: a quick scan, rather than a line-by-line hunt.

▲ **For incomplete statements, restrict the number of blanks to one or two.** If you use too many blanks in an incomplete statement, your students may find it absolutely incomprehensible. For obvious reasons, test-developers describe such multiblank items as "Swiss Cheese" items. Think of the variety of responses students could supply for the following, bizarrely ambiguous example:

A SWISS CHEESE ITEM

Following a decade of Herculean struggles, in the year
_____ , _____ and his partner, _____ ,
finally discovered how to make _____ .
(Answer: ???)

▲ **Make all response-blanks equal in length.** Novice item-writers often vary the lengths of their response-blanks to better match the correct answers they're seeking. It just looks nicer that way. To avoid supplying your students with unintended clues, always stick with response blanks of uniform length.

▲ **Supply sufficient answer space.** Yes, the idea is to solicit *short* answers, but be sure you give your students adequate room to provide the sought-for word or phrase. Don't forget to factor in the size of students' handwriting. Your average 2nd grader, for example, will need more space per word than your average 9th grader.

Essay Items

Essay items have been around for so long that it's a good bet Socrates once asked Plato to describe Greek-style democracy in an essay of at least 500 words. I suspect that Plato's essay would have satisfied any of today's content standards dealing with written communication, not to mention a few content standards dealing with social studies. And that's one reason essay items have endured for so long in our classrooms: They are very flexible and can be used to measure students' mastery of all sorts of truly worthwhile curricular aims.

Advantages and Disadvantages

As an assessment tactic to measure truly sophisticated types of student learning, essay items do a terrific job. If you teach high school biology and you want your students to carry out a carefully reasoned analysis of creationism versus evolutionism as alternative explanations for the origin of life, asking students to respond to an essay item can put them, at least cognitively, smack in the middle of that complex issue.

Essay items also give students a great opportunity to display their composition skills. Indeed, for more than two decades, most of the statewide tests taken by U.S. students have required the composition of original essays on assigned topics such as "a persuasive essay on Topic *X*" or "a narrative essay on Topic *Y*." Referred to as *writing samples*, these essay-writing tasks have been instrumental in altering the way that many teachers provide composition instruction.

Essay items have two real shortcomings: (1) *the time required to score students' essays* and (2) *the potential inaccuracies associated with that scoring.* There's really no way for classroom teachers to get around the time-requirement problem, but recent research in the electronic scanning and scoring of students' essays for large-scale assessments suggests that we are getting quite close to computer-based scoring of essays. With respect to the second problem, inaccurate scoring, we have learned from efforts to evaluate essays in statewide and national tests that it is possible to do so with a remarkable degree of accuracy, provided that sufficient resources are committed to the effort and well-trained scoring personnel are in place. And thanks to the use of rubrics, which I'll get to in a page or two, even classroom teachers can go a long way toward making their own scoring of essays more precise. It can be tricky, though, as students' compositional abilities can sometimes obscure their mastery of the curricular aim the item is intended to reveal. For example, Shelley knows the content, but she cannot express herself, or her knowledge, very well in writing; Dan, on the other hand, doesn't know the content but can fake it through very skillful writing. Rubrics are one way to keep a student's ability or inability to spin out a compelling composition from deluding you into an incorrect inference about that student's knowledge or skill.

Item-Writing Rules

There are five rules that classroom teachers really need to follow when constructing essay items.

▲ **Structure items so that the student's task is explicitly circumscribed.** Phrase your essay items so that students will have no doubt about the response you're seeking. Don't hesitate to add details to eliminate ambiguity. Consider the following two items. One of them is likely to leave far too much uncertainty in the test-taker's mind and, as a result, is unlikely to provide evidence about the particular educational variables the item-writer is (clumsily) looking to uncover.

A DREADFULLY AMBIGUOUS ITEM

Discuss youth groups in Europe.

A DELIGHTFULLY CIRCUMSCRIBED ITEM

Describe, in 400–600 words, how the rulers of Nazi Germany in the 1930s used the Hitler Youth Movement to solidify the Nazi political position.

▲ **For each question, specify the point value, an acceptable response-length, and a recommended time allocation.** What this second rule tries to do is give students the information they need to respond appropriately to an essay item. The less guessing that your students are obliged to do about how they're supposed to respond, the less likely it is that you'll get lots of off-the-wall essays that don't give you the evidence you need. Here's an example of how you might tie down some otherwise imponderables and give your students a better chance to show you what you're interested in finding out.

SUITABLE SPECIFICITY

What do you believe is an appropriate U.S. policy regarding the control of global warming? Include in your response at least two concrete activities that would occur if your recommended policy were implemented. (Value: 20 points; Length: 200–300 words; Recommended Response Time: 20 minutes)

▲ **Employ more questions requiring shorter answers rather than fewer questions requiring longer answers.** This rule is intended to foster better content sampling in a test's essay items. With only one or two items on a test, chances are awfully good that your items may miss your students' areas of content mastery or nonmastery. For instance, if a student hasn't properly studied the content for one item in a three-item essay test, that's one-third of the exam already scuttled.

▲ **Don't employ optional questions.** I know that teachers love to give students options because choice tends to support positive student engagement. Yet, when students can choose their essay items from several options, you really end up with *different* tests, unsuitable for comparison. For this reason, I recommend sticking with non-optionality. It is always *theoretically* possible for teachers to create two or more "equidifficult" items to assess mastery of the same curricular aim. But in the real word of schooling, a teacher who can whip up two or more constructed-response items that are equivalent in difficulty is most likely an extraterrestrial in hiding. Items that aren't really equi-difficult lead to students taking on noncomparable challenges.

▲ **Gauge a question's quality by creating a trial response to the item.** A great way to determine if your essay items are really going to get at the responses you want is to actually try writing a response to the item, much as a student might do. And you can expect that kind of payoff even if you make your trial response only "in your head" instead of on paper.

Rubrics: Not All Are Created Equal

I have indicated that a significant shortcoming of constructed-response tests, and of essay items in particular, is the potential inaccuracy of scoring. A properly fashioned rubric can go a long way toward remedying that deficit. And even more importantly, a properly fashioned rubric can help teachers teach much more effectively and help students learn much more effectively, too. In short, the instructional payoffs of properly fashioned rubrics may actually exceed their assessment dividends. However, and this is an important point for you to remember, *not all rubrics are properly fashioned*. Some are wonderful, and some are worthless. You must be able to tell the difference.

What Is a Rubric, Anyway?

A *rubric* is a scoring guide that's intended to help those who must score students' responses to constructed-response items. You might be wondering why it is that measurement people chose to use a cryptic word such as "rubric" instead of the more intuitively understandable "scoring guide." My answer is that *all* specialist fields love to have their own special terminology, and "rubric" is sufficiently opaque to be a terrific turn-on to the measurement community.

The most important component in any rubric is the rubric's *evaluative criteria*, which are the factors a scorer considers when determining the quality of a student's response. For example, one evaluative criterion in an essay-scoring rubric might be the organization of the essay. Evaluative criteria are truly the guts of any rubric, because they lay out what it is that distinguishes students' winning responses from their weak ones.

A second key ingredient in a rubric is a set of *quality definitions* that accompany each evaluative criterion. These quality definitions spell out what is needed, with respect to each evaluative criterion, for a student's response to receive a high rating versus a low rating on that criterion. A quality definition for an evaluative criterion like "essay organization" might identify the types of organizational structures that are acceptable and those that aren't. The mission of a rubric's quality definitions is to reduce the likelihood that the rubric's evaluative criteria will be misunderstood.

Finally, a rubric should set forth a *scoring strategy* that indicates how a scorer should use the evaluative criteria and their quality definitions. There are two main contenders, as far as scoring strategy is concerned. A *holistic* scoring strategy signifies that the scorer must attend to how well a student's response satisfies all the evaluative criteria in the interest of forming a general, overall evaluation of the response based on all criteria considered in concert. In contrast, an *analytic* approach to scoring requires a scorer to make a criterion-by-criterion judgment for each of the evaluative criteria, and then amalgamate those per-criterion ratings into a final score (this is often done via a set of predetermined, possibly numerical, rules).

The most widespread use of rubrics occurs with respect to the scoring of students' writing samples. In large-scale scoring operations, holistic scoring is usually the preferred approach because it is faster and, hence, less expensive. However, analytic scoring is clearly more diagnostic, as it permits the calculation of a student's per-criterion performance. Some states keep costs down by scoring all student writing samples holistically first, then scoring only "failing" responses analytically.

Early rubrics used by educators in the United States were intended to help score students' writing samples. Although there were surely some qualitative differences among those rubrics, for the most part they all worked remarkably well. Not only could different scorers score the same writing samples and come up with similar appraisals, but the evaluative criteria in those early rubrics were instructionally addressable. Thus, teachers could use each evaluative criterion to teach their students precisely how their writing samples would be judged. Indeed, students' familiarity with the evaluative criteria contained in those writing sample rubrics meant they could critique their own compositions and those of their classmates as a component of instruction.

To this day, most writing sample rubrics contribute wonderfully to accurate scoring and successful instruction. Unfortunately, many teachers have come to believe that *any* rubric will lead to those twin dividends. As you're about to see, that just isn't so.

Reprehensible Rubrics

I've identified three kinds of rubrics that are far from properly fashioned if the objective is both evaluative accuracy and instructional benefit. They are (1) *task-specific rubrics*, (2) *hypergeneral rubrics,* and (3) *dysfunctionally detailed rubrics;* each of these reprehensible rubrics takes its name chiefly from the type of evaluative criteria it contains. Let's take a closer look to see where the failings lie.

Task-specific rubrics. This type of rubric contains evaluative criteria that refer to the *particular task* that the student has been asked to perform, not the *skill* that task was created to represent. For example, one pivotal skill in science class might be the ability to understand and then explain how certain scientifically rooted processes function. If an essay item in a science class asked students to explain how a vacuum thermos works, a task-specific rubric's evaluative criteria would help *only* in the scoring of responses to that *specific* vacuum thermos–explaining task. The rubric's evaluative criteria, focused exclusively on the particular task, would have no relevance to the evaluation of students' responses to other tasks representing the cognitive skill being measured. Task-specific rubrics don't help teachers teach and they don't help students learn. They are way too *specific!*

Hypergeneral rubrics. A second type of reprehensible rubric is one whose evaluative criteria are so very, very general that the only thing we really know after consulting the rubric is something such as "a good response is . . . good" and "a bad response is the opposite"! To illustrate, in recent years, I have seen many hypergeneral rubrics that describe "distinguished" student responses in a manner similar to this: "A complete and fully accurate response to the task posed, presented in a particularly clear and well-written manner." Hypergeneral rubrics provide little more clarity to teachers and students than what's generally implied by an *A* through *F* grading system. Hypergeneral rubrics don't help teachers teach, and they don't help students learn. They are way too *general!*

Dysfunctionally detailed rubrics. Finally, there are the rubrics that have loads and loads of evaluative criteria, each with its own extremely detailed set of quality descriptions. These rubrics are just too blinking long. Because few teachers and students have the patience or time to wade through rubrics of this type, these rubrics don't help teachers teach or students learn. They are, as you have already guessed, way too *detailed!*

A Skill-Focused Rubric: The Kind You Want

For accurate evaluation of constructed-response tests and to provide instructional benefits, you need a rubric that deals with the *skill* being tapped by that test. These *skill-focused rubrics* are exemplified by the early rubrics used to score U.S. students' writing samples. Here's what you'll find in a properly designed skill-focused rubric:

▲ **It includes only a handful of evaluative criteria.** Skill-focused rubrics incorporate only the most important evaluative factors to be used in appraising a student's performance. This way, teachers and students can remain attentive to a modest number of super-important evaluative criteria, rather than being overwhelmed or sidetracked.

▲ **It reflects something teachable.** Teachers need to be able to *teach* students to master an important skill. Thus, each evaluative criterion on a good skill-focused rubric should be included only after an affirmative answer is given to this question: "Can I get my students to be able to use this evaluative criterion in judging their own mastery of the skill I'm teaching them?"

▲ **All the evaluative criteria are applicable to any skill-reflective task.** If this condition is satisfied, of course, it is impossible for the rubric to be task-specific. For example, if a student's impromptu speech is being evaluated with a skill-focused rubric, the evaluative criteria of "good eye contact" will apply to any topic the student is asked to speak about, whether it's "My Fun Summer" or "How to Contact the City Council."

▲ **It is concise.** Brevity is the best way to ensure that a rubric is read and used by both teachers and students. Ideally, each evaluative criterion should have a brief, descriptive label. And, as long as we're going for ideal, it usually makes sense for the teacher to conjure up a short, plain-talk student version of any decent skill-focused rubric.

Illustrative Evaluative Criteria

If you've put two and two together, you've come to the conclusion that a rubric's instructional quality usually hinges chiefly on the way that its evaluative criteria are given. Figure 7.1 clarifies how it is that those criteria can help or hinder a teacher's instructional thinking. In it, you'll see three different types of evaluative criteria: one criterion each from a hypergeneral rubric, a task-specific rubric, and a skill-focused rubric. All three focus on the same variable: students' organization of a narrative essay.

7.1   ILLUSTRATIVE EVALUATIVE CRITERIA FOR THREE KINDS OF RUBRICS

Introduction: A 6th grade class (fictional) has been visited by a group of local fire-fighters. The teacher asks the students to compose a narrative essay recounting the previous day's visit. *Organization* is one of the key evaluative criteria in the rubric that the teacher routinely uses to appraise students' compositions. Presented below are three ways of describing that criterion:

A Hypergeneral Rubric
Organization: "Superior" essays are those in which the essay's content has been arranged in a genuinely excellent manner, whereas "inferior" essays are those that display altogether inadequate organization. An "adequate" essay is one that repre-sents a lower organizational quality than a superior essay, but a higher organiza-tional quality than an inferior essay.

A Task-Specific Rubric
Organization: "Superior" essays will (1) commence with a recounting of the partic-ular rationale for home fire-escape plans that the local firefighters presented, then (2) follow up with a description of the six elements in home-safety plans in the order that those elements were described, and (3) conclude by citing at least three of the life-death safety statistics the firefighters provided at the close of their class-room visit. Departures from these three organizational elements will result in lower evaluations of essays.

A Skill-Focused Rubric
Organization: Two aspects of organization will be employed in the appraisal of stu-dents' narrative essays, namely, *overall structure* and *sequence.* To earn maximum credit, an essay must embody an overall structure containing an introduction, a body, and a conclusion. The content of the body of the essay must be sequenced in a reasonable manner, for instance, in a chronological, logical, or order-of-importance sequence.

Notice that the hypergeneral evaluative criterion offers little insight into what the organization of the student's essay must be like other than "good." Instructionally, that's not much to go on. The task-specific evaluative criterion would work well for evaluating students' narrative essays about this particular firefighters' visit to class, but how many times would a student need to write a narrative essay on that specific topic? Finally, the skill-focused evaluative criterion isolates two organizational features: a reasonable sequence and the need for an "introduction-body-conclusion" structure. Those two organizational elements are not only teachable, but they are also applicable to a host of narrative essays.

In short, you'll find that skill-focused rubrics can be used not only to score your students' responses to constructed-response tests, but also to guide both you and your students toward students' mastery of the skill being assessed. Skill-focused rubrics help teachers teach; they help students learn. They go a long way toward neutralizing the drawbacks of constructed-response assessments while maximizing the advantages.

Special Variants of Constructed-Response Assessment

Before we close the primer on constructed-response tests, I want to address a couple of alternative forms of constructive response evaluation, both of which have become increasingly prominent in recent years: *performance assessment* and *portfolio assessment.*

Performance Assessment

Educators differ in their definitions of what a performance assessment is. Some educators believe that *any kind of constructed response* constitutes a performance test. Those folks are in the minority. Most educators regard performance assessment as an attempt to measure a student's mastery of a high-level, sometimes quite sophisticated skill through the use of fairly elaborate constructed-response items and a rubric. Performance tests always present a *task* to students. In the case of evaluating students' written communication skills, that task might be to "write a 500-word narrative essay." (Assessment folks call the tasks on writing tests *prompts.*) And the more that the student's assessment task resembles the tasks to be performed by people in real life, the more likely it is that the test will be labeled a performance assessment.

An example of a performance assessment in social studies might be for each student to (1) come up with a current-day problem that could be solved by drawing directly on historical lessons; (2) prepare a 3,000-word written report describing the applicability of the historical lessons to the current-day problem; and finally, (3) present a 10-minute oral report in class describing the student's key conclusions. No one would dispute that this sort of a problem presents students with a much more difficult task to tackle than choosing between *true* and *false* responses in a test composed of binary-choice items.

There are a couple of drawbacks to performance assessments, one obvious and the other more subtle. The obvious one is time. This kind of assessment requires a significant time investment from teachers (designing a multistep performance task, developing an evaluative rubric, and applying the evaluative rubric to the performance) and from students (preparing for the performance and the performance itself). A less obvious but more serious obstacle for those who advocate the use of performance assessment is the problem of generalizability. How many performance tests do students need to complete before the teacher can come up with valid inferences about their generalizable skill-mastery? Will one well-written persuasive essay be enough to determine the degree to which a particular student has mastered the skill of writing persuasive essays? How many reports about the use of history-based lessons are needed before a teacher can say that a student really is able to employ lessons from past historical events to deal with current-day problems?

The research evidence related to this issue is not encouraging. Empirical investigations suggest that teachers would be obliged to give students *many* performance assessments before arriving at a truly accurate interpretation about a student's skill-mastery (Linn & Burton, 1994). "Many performance assessments" translates into even more planning and classroom time. On practical grounds, therefore, teachers need to be very selective in their use of this exciting, but time-consuming assessment approach. I recommend reserving performance assessments for only the most significant of your high-priority curricular aims.

Portfolio Assessment

Let's close out the chapter with a quick look at another special sort of constructed-response measurement: *portfolio assessment.* A portfolio is a collection of one's work. Essentially, portfolio assessment requires students to continually collect and evaluate their ongoing work for the purpose of improving the skills they need to create such work. Language arts portfolios, usually writing portfolios or journals, are the example cited most often; however, portfolio assessment can be used to assess the student's evolving mastery of many kinds of skills in many different subject areas.

Suppose Mr. Miller, a 5th grade teacher, is targeting his students' abilities to write brief multiparagraph compositions. Mr. Miller sets aside a place in the classroom (perhaps a file cabinet) where students, using teacher-supplied folders, collect and critique the compositions they create throughout the entire school year. Working with his 5th graders to decide what the suitable qualities of good compositions are, Mr. Miller creates a skill-focused rubric students will use to critique their own writing. When students evaluate a composition, they attach a dated, filled-in rubric form. Students also engage in a fair amount of peer critique, using the same skill-focused rubric to review each other's compositions. Every month, Mr. Miller holds a brief portfolio conference with each student to review the student's current work and to decide collaboratively on directions for improvement. Mr. Miller also calls on parents to participate in those portfolio conferences at least once per semester. The emphasis is always on *improving* students' abilities to evaluate their own multiparagraph compositions in these "working" portfolios. At the end of the year, each student selects a best-work set of compositions, and these "showcase" portfolios are then taken home to students' parents.

As you can see, given such a continuing emphasis on the enhancement of students' self-appraisal skills, there is a considerable likelihood that portfolio assessment will yield major payoffs for students. And teachers who have used portfolios agree with their power as a combined assessment and instruction strategy.

But those same teachers, if they are honest, will also point out that staying abreast of students' portfolios and carrying out periodic portfolio conferences is really time-consuming. Be sure to consider the time-consumption drawback carefully before diving headfirst into the portfolio pool.

INSTRUCTIONALLY FOCUSED TESTING TIPS

• Understand the relative strengths of constructed-response items and selected-response items.

• Become familiar with the advantages and disadvantages of short-answer and essay items.

• Make certain to follow experience-based rules for creating short-answer and essay items.

• When scoring students' responses to constructed-response tests, employ skill-focused scoring rubrics rather than rubrics that are task specific, hypergeneral, or dysfunctionally detailed.

• Recognize both the pros and cons associated with performance testing and portfolio assessment.

Recommended Resources

Andrade, H. G. (2000, February). Using rubrics to promote thinking and learning. *Educational Leadership, 57*(5), 13–18.

Eisner, E. W. (1999, May). The uses and limits of performance assessment. *Phi Delta Kappan, 80*(9), 658–660.

Letts, N., Kallick, B., Davis, H. B., & Martin-Kniep, G. (Presenters). (1999). *Portfolios: A guide for students and teachers* [Audiotape]. Alexandria, VA: Association for Supervision and Curriculum Development.

Linn, R. L., & Burton, E. (1994). Performance-based assessment: Implications of task specificity. *Educational measurement: Issues and practice, 13*(1), 5–8, 15.

Mabry, L. (1999, May). Writing to the rubric: Lingering effects of traditional standardized testing on direct writing assessment. *Phi Delta Kappan, 80*(9), 673–679.

McMillan, J. H. (2001). *Classroom assessment: Principles and practice for effective instruction* (2nd ed.). Boston: Allyn & Bacon.

Northwest Regional Educational Laboratory. (1991). *Developing assessments based on observation and judgment* [Videotape]. Los Angeles: IOX Assessment Associates.

Pollock, J. (Presenter). (1996). *Designing authentic tasks and scoring rubrics* [Audiotape]. Alexandria, VA: Association for Supervision and Curriculum Development.

Popham, W. J. (Program Consultant). (1996). *Creating challenging classroom tests: When students CONSTRUCT their responses* [Videotape]. Los Angeles: IOX Assessment Associates.

Popham, W. J. (Program Consultant). (1998). *The role of rubrics in classroom assessment* [Videotape]. Los Angeles: IOX Assessment Associates.

Stiggins, R. J. (Program Consultant). (1996). *Assessing reasoning in the classroom* [Videotape]. Portland, OR: Assessment Training Institute.

Wiggins, G., Stiggins, R. J., Moses, M., & LeMahieu, P. (Program Consultants). (1991). *Redesigning assessment: Portfolios* [Videotape]. Alexandria, VA: Association for Supervision and Curriculum Development.

The Value of
Affective Assessment

AFFECT DESCRIBES A MEDLEY OF NONCOGNITIVE VARIABLES SUCH AS A PERSON'S attitudes, interests, and values. To educators, student affect is terribly important. If teachers can help their students acquire positive attitudes toward learning or can help their students derive more satisfaction from reading, then those teachers will have done something wonderful. Indeed, if I were pushed to register a preference for either affective or cognitive outcomes, I'd definitely opt for affect.

The reasons are simple: Children who love learning will keep on learning. Children who enjoy reading will keep on reading even when they aren't "required" to read. On the flip side, think about math teachers who get their students to be super-skilled in math and yet, in the process, lead a number of those students to detest all things mathematical. I would *not* regard such teachers as successful. A teacher who quashes students' positive regard for learning is doing something awful.

Why Assess Affect?

The first reason that I believe educators should be interested in assessing affective variables is because those variables are excellent predictors of students' future behavior. For example, if students learn to enjoy giving speeches while they're in school, chances are that they will be better at public speaking later in life, going on to communicate well in work environments, in community politics, and as members of their children's parent-teacher associations.

The relationship between assessments of affective variables as predictors of students' subsequent behaviors and those subsequent behaviors is depicted graphically in Figure 8.1. This predictive relationship is rooted in probabilities. Suppose there were 100 high school seniors who, as measured by affective assessments, displayed really positive attitudes toward school and, in particular, toward the act of learning itself. Then suppose there were 100 high school seniors whose affective assessments showed that they hated school and found repugnant anything even mildly linked to learning. Now, in which of the two groups would you expect to find a higher percentage of high schoolers enrolling in some form of postsecondary education? On average, of course, far more of the school-lovers would hop on the postsecondary bus than would their school-hating counterparts.

8.1 | **THE PREDICTIVE NATURE OF STUDENTS' IN-SCHOOL ASSESSED AFFECT**

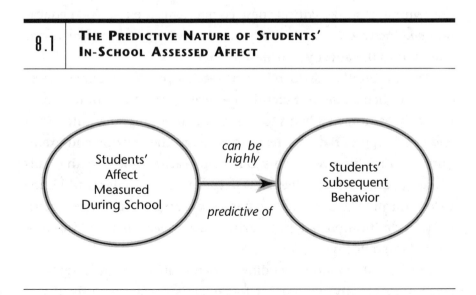

Given that most teachers really *do* care about their students' success in subsequent grade levels and in life thereafter, they can pick up some awfully important insights about their students' future behaviors by employing a bit of affective assessment. Think for a moment about children who dislike school or, more specifically, dislike reading (because of boredom, low skill levels, and so on). These children are *not* likely to read on their own and are likely to go on disliking and avoiding reading in future years. Don't teachers have a professional obligation not only to try to reinforce and enhance positive attitudes, but also to intervene to change negative ones?

Another reason teachers should assess affect is to simply remind themselves that there's more to being a successful teacher than helping students obtain high scores on achievement tests. It has been said that "we measure what we treasure," and it's true. If you set aside classroom time to assess certain attitudes, interests, or values your students possess, you are asserting these things are important— important enough to be worthy of promotion and the targets of instructional attention. The simple act of assessing student affect, especially at the beginning of the school year and at its conclusion, can remind you how critical these components are to a good education *and* increase the odds that you will devote greater instructional attention to the affect you believe matters most.

There is another dividend when teachers devise affective assessments for their students. Much as the creating and examining of conventional assessments helps to clarify cognitive curricular intentions and clarify appropriate means to those ends, the creating and examining of affective assessments can help teachers identify the hallmarks of particular affective targets. (Let's face it, "Students will learn to love learning" is about as fuzzy as a goal can get!) Such assessment-induced clarification can give teachers useful ideas about how to promote those outcomes.

Finally, information regarding students' affect can help teachers teach more effectively on a day-to-day basis. Most obviously, if you discover through affective assessment that your students are really bored and disinterested in the content you're presenting or plan to present, then you can do something to address that problem in tomorrow's lesson.

Which Affect Should Teachers Assess?

Before going much further into the assessment of affect, let me emphasize that teachers need to make sure that any affective variables they assess or attempt to promote instructionally should be *noncontroversial* attitudes, interests, and values. Many parents are understandably wary of schools' intruding on matters they believe should be dealt with within the family. Lots of parents would properly take umbrage if a teacher attempted to influence students' values regarding such issues as abortion or the appropriateness of various lifestyle choices. Here's an easy-to-remember guideline: *Steer clear of any affective variable that would fail to secure endorsement from nearly everyone.*

Still, there are plenty of powerful and noncontroversial affective variables to which teachers can attend:

• Possible *attitude targets* include positive attitudes toward learning, positive attitudes toward self, and positive attitudes toward those who differ from ourselves.

• Possible *interest targets* include interest in specific school subjects, interest in public affairs, and interest in altruistic endeavors.

• Possible *value targets* include honesty, integrity, and justice.

How to Measure Affect: The Self-Report Inventory

Although there are a number of exotic assessment approaches teachers can take to get a fix on students' attitudes, values, and interests (including surreptitious observation and the use of accomplices), the most straightforward, cost-effective way to measure affect in the classroom is to rely on students' anonymous responses to *self-report inventories.* ("Inventory," by the way, is just a fancy label for almost any sort of self-report instrument. If you prefer to use such essentially equivalent synonyms as "survey," "questionnaire," or "report," you're certainly welcome to do so.) In their excellent book about affective assessment, Anderson and Bourke (2000) provide a persuasive argument that, in the real world of schooling, students' affect ought to be measured exclusively through self-report inventories. If you're interested in seeing how they arrive at this conclusion about the merits of self-report assessment, you might want to look at Chapter 3 in their very readable book.

Always Ensure Anonymity

To place any confidence in students' responses to self-report inventories, however, it is imperative that students supply those responses anonymously. Moreover, it is necessary for students to *truly believe* that their responses cannot be traced. Students who suspect otherwise are more apt to make socially desirable responses—responses they believe adults would want them to make. If you hope to collect evidence that will support valid inferences about your students' true attitudes, interests, and values, then anonymity is the only way to go.

Here are several anonymity-enhancement tactics that should help you collect the honest answers you're looking for.

▲ **Stress anonymity in the self-report directions.** Tell your students not to put their names on their inventories. Emphasize that you will not be tracing responses back to the originators and that there are no right or wrong answers. Include these directions on the printed self-report inventories.

▲ **Explain the assessment's rationale.** Make it clear to your students that the purpose of this collection of self-report information is to help you improve your instruction. You are not interested in evaluating them as individuals or as a group.

▲ **Restrict responses to marks.** Tell your students (orally and in the self-report inventory's written directions) that they must make their responses using only checkmarks or X-marks, not words or sentences. If you want to secure anonymous *written* comments from your students, provide a different response form and collect it separately.

Remember, you are attempting to enhance students' perception of true anonymity, and students tend to think that hand-written comments are not only potentially traceable, but apt to be traced. Separate written comments present a far "safer" alternative.

▲ **Provide for anonymous collection.** Direct your students to place their completed inventories in a collection box or have a student (not one of your "favorite" students) collect the completed inventories. Describe your planned collection procedure to students before they begin to respond to the inventory.

▲ **Give students space.** While your students are filling out their affective inventories, refrain from "hovering" so close to them that students think you might be able to see how they are responding. This is a great time for teachers to engage in blissfully restful at-desk sitting.

Always Make Group-Focused Inferences Only

Given the anonymity of these self-report inventories, you may be wondering how you could ever get a fix on an individual student's affective status. Well, the answer's simple: You can't.

In any group of 25–30 students responding to an anonymous self-report affective inventory, there will be a few students who respond too positively and a few who respond too negatively. The teacher's only recourse is to focus on the group's *average* response, allowing the too-positive and too-negative responses to cancel each other. All affective inferences, therefore, must be *group-focused inferences*. Based on self-report inventories, a teacher can conclude with reasonable accuracy how confident a *group* of students are in their oral communication skills. But that teacher cannot conclude anything about *Maria's* confidence in being able to give oral reports, because the risk of that conclusion's invalidity is just too high. Despite understandable temptation to do so, affective inferences should *never* be individually focused.

As another example, based on students' anonymous responses to a self-report affective inventory administered at the beginning of the school year, a teacher might conclude that, "My students appear to be really interested in social studies as a content area, but are quite negative about science." It is these sorts of group-focused inferences that you'll be getting from affective assessments. The purpose of coming up with those sorts of inferences is to help you do a better job of teaching—to help you identify areas of student affect that, based on your students' affective status, you may wish to address instructionally.

Building Affective Inventories for Your Classroom

There are three kinds of affective self-report inventories that teachers can use in their own classrooms: (1) *Likert inventories,* (2) Likert-like *multidimensional inventories,* and (3) *confidence inventories.* Two of the three are particularly suitable for most teachers' needs. Let's take a closer look.

Likert Inventories

The best known and most widely used kind of affective inventory is the Likert inventory, a self-report instrument named after its inventor, who came up with the measurement approach in the early 1930s. Most of us have completed at least a few Likert inventories. The format presents a series of statements (items) to which individuals register the degree of agreement they have for each statement, most commonly "Strongly Agree," "Agree," "Uncertain," "Disagree," and "Strongly Disagree." Respondents might also be asked to register their agreements in other ways such as "True for me," "Not true for me," "Unsure," and so on. Likert inventories for young children usually contain only two or three simple response-options such as "Yes," "No," or "Not Sure." Inventories for older children usually provide four or five response-options per item.

The critical feature of Likert inventories is that they are "unidimensional," meaning that all the statements in a given inventory are designed to collect evidence focused on a *single affective variable*. Examples of a single affective variable might be attitudes toward individuals from ethnic groups other than one's own, interest in scientific phenomena, and valuing of democratic approaches to government. In a typical Likert inventory, you might find 20–30 statements, some reflecting positive responses toward the affective variable being measured and some reflecting negative responses. Figure 8.2 shows an excerpt from a 20-item affective assessment instrument aimed at measuring middle school students' attitudes toward public service or, more specifically, their attitudes toward serving as an elected member of government.

Notice that some of the statements in the Figure 8.2 inventory reflect positive attitudes toward serving in public office and some of the statements represent the opposite. If students were really enthusiastic about seeking elected political office, they would tend to agree with the positive statements and disagree with the negative statements.

To score an inventory like this, you'd assign three points for every agreement with a positive statement or for any disagreement with a negative statement. You'd give two points for any "Uncertain" response. You'd give one point for every disagreement with a positive statement or for any agreement with a negative statement. Scores, then, could range between 60 and 20 for the full 20-item inventory. Higher scores would represent students' more positive attitudes toward serving as an elected public servant.

I like Likert inventories a lot, and I've used them often throughout my career. When teaching a course about educational assessment, I often used some sort of Likert inventory to assess my students' comfort in dealing with assessment-related concepts. Likert inventories have the additional advantage of being relatively easy to construct. However, remember that the characteristic "unidimensionality" of Likert inventories means that they measure only *single* affective variables. In reality, most teachers are likely to be interested in *several* affective variables. For this reason, I think that the creation and use of full-blown, 25-item Likert inventories dealing with a single affective variable usually represents assessment overkill in the classroom environment.

8.2 | A LIKERT INVENTORY EXCERPT

MY ATTITUDES TOWARD ELECTIVE OFFICE

Directions: Presented below are 20 statements dealing with public service. Please read each statement, then indicate whether you agree with that statement, disagree with it, or are uncertain by checking one of the three response boxes for the statement. An example is provided below.

	Agree	Uncertain	Disagree
I like to eat large breakfasts.	☐	☐	✔

(In this example, the person did not like large breakfasts, so checked "Disagree.")

There are no correct or incorrect answers, so please answer honestly. Do not write your name on this inventory. Your responses will be totally anonymous.

Statements   **Your Responses**

	Agree	Uncertain	Disagree
1. Most politicians are dishonest.	☐	☐	☐
2. I would like to be a U.S. senator.	☐	☐	☐
3. Without elected legislators, our society fails.	☐	☐	☐
4. I hope my friends don't enter politics.	☐	☐	☐
5. Today's politicians shape tomorrow's world.	☐	☐	☐

| 19. I will never run for a political office. | ☐ | ☐ | ☐ |
| 20. Democracy loses without elected officials. | ☐ | ☐ | ☐ |

Multidimensional Inventories

What you're looking for when you assess your students' affect is an approximate idea about your students' attitudes, interests, or values. Given the need for only approximations of a student group's affective status, I recommend the use of *multidimensional inventories.* These inventories *look* like Likert inventories, for they ask students to register degrees of agreement with a series of statements. But unlike Likert inventories, the statements in multidimensional inventories often deal with a considerable number of different affective variables. Consider Figure 8.3, and I'll show you what I mean.

The inventory in this figure is intended for students in grades 4–6 and designed to measure seven variables that might interest a classroom teacher, including attitude toward school, attitude toward making oral presentations, and interest in science. Each of those affective variables is measured by two statements, one of which is stated positively and one of which is stated negatively. For example, compare Statement 1 with Statement 14, and Statement 2 with Statement 8.

Based on what we know about content sampling, I realize that it's pretty difficult to place enormous confidence in the results of any sort of two-item assessment. Remember, though, that the goal is to come up with a valid inference about the affective status of the *whole class.* What we're really talking about is a two-item assessment multiplied by the number of students who respond—30 items for a class of 15, for example, 40 items for a class of 20, and so on. If the affective inventory's items are thoughtfully developed, teachers can gain a sufficiently accurate picture regarding the affective status of their students as a group.

If you construct your own multidimensional affective inventories, remember that each variable you want to measure must be represented by two items, one positive and one negative. Moreover, be sure to phrase your inventory statements so that they are moderately positive and moderately negative. This lukewarm approach is necessary to elicit the varied responses that you need to make a two-item

8.3 | A LIKERT-LIKE MULTIDIMENSIONAL INVENTORY

School and Me: An Affective Inventory

Directions: Please indicate how true or untrue the statements in this inventory are for you. Some of the statements are positive; some are negative. Decide if each statement is true for you. There are no right or wrong answers. Please answer honestly. Do not write your name on this inventory. Only make *X* marks. An example is provided below.

Response (one per statement)

Statement	Very true for me.	Not true for me.	I'm not sure.
I enjoy going to the movies.	☐	☒	☐

When you are finished, a student will collect your inventory and place it (and all other completed inventories) in an envelope that we will seal and take directly to the principal's office. Thank you for your help.

Statements — **Your Responses**

Statements	Very true for me.	Not true for me.	I'm not sure.
1. Most of the time, I really like school.	☐	☐	☐
2. I often like to learn about scientific things.	☐	☐	☐
3. I can usually write good reports and stories.	☐	☐	☐
4. I don't like to read.	☐	☐	☐
5. I don't like to give oral reports in class.	☐	☐	☐
6. I think that doing mathematics is fun.	☐	☐	☐
7. I like it when we learn about social studies.	☐	☐	☐
8. I don't want to be a scientist when I'm older.	☐	☐	☐
9. I really don't like to write very much.	☐	☐	☐
10. I like to read books when I have time to do it.	☐	☐	☐
11. I enjoy speaking in front of other students.	☐	☐	☐
12. I dislike doing mathematics problems.	☐	☐	☐
13. When we do social studies, I don't like it.	☐	☐	☐
14. Overall, I really don't enjoy school all that much.	☐	☐	☐

assessment pay off. For instance, Statement 1 in Figure 8.3 says, "Most of the time, I really like school." I'd call that statement moderately positive, wouldn't you? It would be likely to elicit different levels of agreement. Now imagine that statement had read "I adore school every single minute of every school day." No sane student could honestly say that such a super-positive statement was "Very true for me." Super-negative statements are similarly ineffective.

Scoring procedures for multidimensional inventories are pretty much the same as for unidimensional Likert inventories (score negative responses low, positive responses high) with the obvious adjustment that you need to compute a two-item score for each affective variable assessed. Thus, assigning each item a three-point, two-point, or one-point value, the highest score for any two-item assessment would be six points, and the lowest score would be two points.

Confidence Inventories

The final kind of affective assessment device that I want you to consider is called a *confidence inventory*. It describes various sorts of activities a student might be asked to engage in, and then it asks students to identify their confidence level if they were personally required to carry out each such activity. As with other types of classroom affective assessments, a confidence inventory's purpose is to provide teachers with insights that can help them make better instructional decisions.

Let's pause for a moment to consider the relationship between a student's expressed confidence in being able to do something and that student's actual competence. In general, the more competence someone possesses in being able to do something, the more confidence that person will have in his or her ability to do it. Of course, there will obviously be exceptions: competent students who lack confidence and incompetent students who ooze confidence. But it's *likely* that students' confidence regarding Skill X will be positively related to their competence regarding Skill X.

You doubtlessly recognize that for certain of the cognitive skills you routinely promote in your classroom, the difficulties of carrying out a full-blown assessment may sometimes be substantial. Think about how difficult it is to get an accurate measurement of your students' skill in collaborative, small-group problem solving. Coming up with suitable assessments of a complex skill like this can be a genuine pain. These are the situations in which confidence inventories can be really valuable, as they can serve as proxies for students' actual, hard-to-measure skills. Remember, though, as for all affective assessments, your inventory-based inferences must focus on your entire class, not on individual students.

Figure 8.4 shows an illustrative confidence inventory intended for upper-grade elementary students. As this inventory deals exclusively with language arts, we will assume that the fictional teacher who developed it was chiefly interested in students' confidence regarding their oral and written communication skills. Notice that all the activities in the inventory are things that students might become more confident about doing over time, provided that their teacher's instruction successfully boosted their oral and written communication skills. Clearly, if you would like to use this sort of inventory in your own classroom, you would need to select activities specifically related to your own instructional concerns.

Notice that this particular confidence inventory includes four possible responses for each of the activities. There could be more response-options or fewer, just as long as the scorer assigns higher point values to the more-confident responses. So, for example, awarding points on a 4-3-2-1 basis, the highest overall score a student could make on this particular 10-item inventory would be 40. If the teacher using this inventory was interested in computing a separate score for oral communication skills (addressed in Items 1, 3, 4, 6, and 9) and written communication skills (addressed in Items 2, 5, 7, 8, and 10), it could be easily done.

8.4 | A CONFIDENCE INVENTORY

Language Arts Confidence Inventory

Directions: This inventory was designed to inform your teacher about the confidence that you and your classmates have in speaking and writing. Its purpose is to help your teacher do a better job. Below, there are 10 statements describing particular activities. Please look at each activity and then imagine that you had to carry out that activity. For each activity, indicate the level of confidence you would have in your ability to do it. Circle only one response for each activity. An example is provided below.

VC = Very Confident   LC = A Little Confident
FC = Fairly Confident   NC = Not Confident at All

Activities	**Your Response**			
Suppose you were asked to . . .	**How confident would you be?**			
Operate a film projector in a theater.	VC	FC	(LC)	NC

Do not write your name on this inventory. There are no "right" or "wrong" answers. Please respond honestly.

Activities	**Your Response**			
Suppose you were asked to . . .	**How confident would you be?**			
1. write a friendly letter to an English-speaking but unknown student in another country.	VC	FC	LC	NC
2. give a 5-minute speech to your classmates about a recent vacation.	VC	FC	LC	NC
3. compose an original *narrative* essay of 500–700 words.	VC	FC	LC	NC
4. compose an original *persuasive* essay of 500–700 words.	VC	FC	LC	NC
5. explain to a classmate how an oral report should be organized.	VC	FC	LC	NC
6. use a computer to compose a short written report.	VC	FC	LC	NC
7. answer a teacher's question aloud in class when you know the answer.	VC	FC	LC	NC
8. disagree aloud, politely but firmly, with a classmate about an issue that the class is studying.	VC	FC	LC	NC
9. write a short essay of 500 words with *no* errors in spelling, punctuation, or usage.	VC	FC	LC	NC
10. give a two-minute impromptu speech in front of the class, without any preparation.	VC	FC	LC	NC

Thank you for completing this confidence inventory.

For purposes of instructional decision making, the most useful scoring approach is often a per-item average for the entire class. That's because each of the activities in the inventory describes a task that you could teach your students how to tackle. Students' responses to content-focused confidence inventories can also help teachers decide how much time they should devote to teaching to such content. A teacher might choose to devote less instructional time to skills and knowledge in which students expressed great confidence and more instructional time to skills and knowledge about which students were less confident.

Finally, of course, pre-assessment/postassessment comparisons of per-item class averages from confidence inventories can be extremely illuminating to teachers trying to get a handle on how well they are teaching. An increase in students' perceptions of their abilities from the start of the school year to its conclusion can really reflect favorably on a teacher's instruction. In Chapter 11, we'll go into this in more detail.

I really hope that you give affective assessment a try in your own classroom. Your students will benefit now and in the years to come.

INSTRUCTIONALLY FOCUSED TESTING TIPS

- Give serious consideration to the assessment of student affect in your own classroom.
- Measure—and deal instructionally—only with noncontroversial attitudes, interests, or values.
- Assess your students' affect using anonymous, self-report inventories.
- Focus all assessment-based inferences regarding students' affect on groups, not individual students.
- Recognize that the assessment of affect will typically sensitize you to the importance of giving instructional attention to students' affect.

Recommended Resources

Anderson, L. W., & Bourke, S. F. (2000). *Assessing affective characteristics in the schools* (2nd ed.). Mahwah, NJ: Lawrence Erlbaum Associates.

Kohn, A. (1997, February). How not to teach values: A critical look at character education. *Phi Delta Kappan, 78*(6), 428–439.

Popham, W. J. (2000). *Modern educational measurement: Practical guidelines for educational leaders* (3rd ed.). Boston: Allyn & Bacon.

Popham, W. J. (2002). *Classroom assessment: What teachers need to know* (3rd ed.). Boston: Allyn & Bacon.

Popham, W. J. (Program Consultant). (1997). *Assessing student attitudes: A key to increasing achievement* [Videotape]. Los Angeles: IOX Assessment Associates.

Popham, W. J. (Program Consultant). (1997). *Improving instruction: Start with student attitudes* [Videotape]. Los Angeles: IOX Assessment Associates.

Uses and Misuses of Standardized Achievement Tests

9

IN THE SPRING OF MY FIRST FULL YEAR OF TEACHING, I ADMINISTERED MY FIRST nationally standardized achievement test. We set aside an hour, our high school's juniors took the test, and we received the score-reports the following fall. I looked over the results to see which of my students had earned high-percentile scores and which had earned low-percentile scores. But, because ours was a small high school with only about 35 students per grade level, I had already discovered which of my students performed well on tests. The standardized test's results yielded no surprises.

Our school district required us to give this test every year, and we routinely mailed all students' score-reports to their parents. As far as I can recall, no parent ever contacted me, the school's principal, or any other teachers about a child's standardized test scores. Why would they? There was nothing riding on the results. Our low-scoring students were not held back a grade level, denied diplomas, or forced to take summer school classes. And no citizen of our rural Oregon town ever tried to evaluate our school's success on the basis of its students' performances on those standardized achievement tests. Those tests, in contrast to today's high-stakes tests, were genuinely *no-stakes* tests. Things have really changed.

Standardized Achievement Tests as *the* Evaluative Yardstick

In the United States today, most citizens regard students' performances on standardized achievement tests as the definitive indicator of school quality. These test scores, published in newspapers, monitored by district administrators and state departments of education, and reported to the federal government, mark school staffs as either successful or unsuccessful. Schools whose students score well on standardized achievement tests are often singled out for applause or, increasingly, given significant monetary rewards. On the flip side of the evaluative coin, schools whose students score too low on standardized tests are singled out for intensive staff development. If test scores do not improve "sufficiently" after substantial staff-development efforts, the schools can be taken over by for-profit corporations or, in some instances, simply closed down altogether.

If you think the consequences of low standardized test scores are considerable now, just wait until NCLB's adequate yearly progress requirements kick in. The NCLB Act requires schools to promote their students' *adequate yearly progress* (AYP) according to a state-determined time schedule. Schools that fail to get sufficient numbers of their students to make AYP (as measured by statewide tests tied to challenging content standards) will be labeled "low performing." After two years of low performance, schools and districts that receive NCLB Title I funds will be subject to a whole series of negative sanctions. For instance, if a school fails to achieve its AYP targets for two consecutive years, parents of children in the school will be permitted to transfer their children to a nonfailing district school—with transportation costs picked up by the district. After another year of missing AYP requirements, the school will be required to supply its students with supplemental instruction, such as tutoring sessions. Unfortunately, the increasing evaluative significance of standardized achievement tests and the resulting pressure on teachers to *raise* their students' test scores are contributing to a number of educationally indefensible practices now seen with increasing frequency. Perhaps the most obvious fallout of the score-boosting frenzy is *curricular reductionism,* wherein teachers have chosen (or have been directed) to give short shrift to any content not assessed on standardized achievement tests. In locales where this kind of curricular shortsightedness is rampant, students simply aren't being given an opportunity to learn the things they should be learning.

A second by-product is a dramatic increase in the amount of *drudgery drilling* in classrooms. Students are required to devote substantial chunks of their school day to relentless, often mind-numbing practice on items similar to those they will encounter on a standardized test. Such drilling can, of course, rapidly extinguish any joy that students might derive either from school or from learning itself. Remember the previous chapter's discussion of affect? Well, today's ubiquitous test-preparation "drill and kill" sessions can quickly destroy the positive attitude toward school that children really ought to have.

Finally, as a result of the enormous pressure on educators to improve students' test scores, we have seen far too many instances of *improper test preparation* or *improper test administration.* In some cases, students have been given test-preparation practice sessions based on the very same items they will encounter on the "real" test. In other instances, students have been given substantially more time to complete a standardized test than is stipulated. (Standardized tests administered in a nonstandardized manner are, of course, no longer standardized.) There are even cases in which students' answer sheets have been massively "refined" by educators prior to the official submission of those answer sheets to a state-designated scoring firm. Obviously, this sort of unethical conduct by educators sends an inappropriate message to students. Thankfully, such conduct is still relatively rare.

It is because the widespread use of standardized achievement tests as the dominant evaluative school-quality yardstick has led to increasingly frequent instances of curricular reductionism, drudgery drilling, and improper test preparation or test administration that I believe today's teachers really need to learn *more* about the uses and misuses of standardized tests. I'll be up-front about my point of view: The primary use of standardized achievement tests today—to evaluate school and teacher quality—is a *misuse*. It is mistaken. It is just plain wrong.

The Measurement Mission of Standardized Achievement Tests

A *standardized* test is any assessment device that's administered and scored in a standard, predetermined manner. Earlier in this book, I explained that *achievement* tests (such as the Stanford Achievement Tests) attempt to measure students' skills and knowledge, whereas *aptitude* tests (such as the ACT and SAT) attempt to predict students' success in some subsequent academic setting. Actually, in a bygone era, educators used to consider aptitude tests "group intelligence" tests. That interpretation has long since gone by the wayside, as it conveys the impression that intelligence is an immutable commodity. Interestingly, even the term "aptitude" has become rather unfashionable. Several years ago, the distributors of the highly esteemed SAT decided to change the official name of their exam from the "Scholastic *Aptitude* Test" to the "Scholastic *Assessment* Test." Their current preference, though, is to use the acronym only: SAT. One suspects that this words-to-letters transformation is an effort to avoid using the term *aptitude*. From a marketing perspective, the letters-only approach may have real merit. Consider how Kentucky Fried Chicken successfully reinvented itself as "KFC."

At any rate, a *standardized achievement test* is designed to measure a student's relative ability to answer the test's items. A student's score is compared to the scores of a carefully selected group of previous test-takers known as the test's *norm group*. Based on these comparisons, we can discover that Sally scored at the 92nd percentile (meaning that Sally outperformed 92 percent of the students in the norm group), while Billy scored at the 13th percentile (meaning that Billy's score only topped 13 percent of the scores earned by students in the norm group).

Such relative comparisons can be useful to both teachers and parents. If a 4th grade teacher discovers that a student has earned an 87th percentile score on a standardized language arts achievement test, but only a 23rd percentile score in a standardized mathematics achievement test, this suggests that some serious instructional attention should be directed toward boosting the student's mathematics moxie. Parents can benefit from such comparative test-based results because these results do serve to identify a child's relative strengths and weaknesses.

This ability to provide accurate, fine-grained comparisons between the scores of a current test-taker and the scores of those previous test-takers who constitute the test's norm group is the cornerstone of standardized achievement testing and has been since standardized testing's origins in the early 20th century. We refer to these comparative test-based interpretations as *norm-referenced* interpretations because we "reference" a student's test score back to the scores of the test's norm group and, thereby, give the student's score meaning. Raw test scores all by themselves are really quite uninterpretable.

In order for a standardized test to permit fine-grained, norm-referenced inferences about a given student's performance, however, it is necessary for the test to produce sufficient *score-spread* (technically referred to as test score *variance*). If the scores yielded by a standardized test were all bunched together within a few points of each other, then precise comparisons among students' scores would be impossible. The production of adequate score-spread, therefore, is imperative for the creators of traditional standardized achievement tests. But it is this quest for score-spread that renders such tests unsuitable for the evaluation of school and teacher quality. Let's see why.

Test Design Features Contributing to Score-Spread . . . and *Inhibiting* Evaluation of Educational Effectiveness

In subsequent sections of this chapter, I am going to be taking a slap or two at standardized achievement tests when they're used to evaluate schools. I'll be disparaging this sort of test use not because the tests themselves are tawdry. To the contrary, I regard traditional standardized achievement tests as first-rate assessment tools when they are used for an appropriate purpose. Nor do I want to imply that the designers of these tests are malevolent measurement monsters out to mislabel students or schools. If we discover that a surgical scalpel has been used as a weapon during an assault, that doesn't mean the firm that manufactured the scalpel is at fault. It's just a case of a tool being used for the wrong purpose. This is just what's happening with the use of standardized tests, created to permit comparisons among students but misapplied to assess educational effectiveness.

An Emphasis on Mid-Difficulty Items

Because most standardized tests are built to be administered in about an hour or so (otherwise, students would become restless or, worse, openly rebellious), the developers of such tests must be very judicious in the kinds of items they select. Their goal is to get maximum score-spread from the fewest number of items and still measure all the required variables.

Statistically, test items that produce the maximum score-spread are those that will be answered correctly by roughly *half* of the test-takers. The testing term *p-value* indicates the percentage of students who answer an item correctly. To create the ample score-spread necessary for precise comparison, test developers select the vast majority of their items so that those items have *p*-values of between .40 and .60—that is, the items were answered correctly by between 40 percent and 60 percent of test-takers when the under-development items were tried out during early field tests.

What the developers of standardized tests resolutely avoid are test items that have extremely low or extremely high p-values. Such items are viewed as space-wasters because they don't "do their share" to spread out students' scores. Accordingly, most of these items are jettisoned before a test is released. And, as a test is revised (which typically takes place every half-dozen years or so), the developers will look at data based on how real test-takers have actually responded. They'll then replace almost all items with p-values that are very high or very low with items that have mid-range p-values, more friendly to score-spread.

Here's the catch: The avoidance of items in the high p-value ranges (p-values of .80 or .90) tends to reduce the ability of standardized achievement tests to detect truly effective instruction. Think about it. Items with high p-values indicate that most students possess the knowledge or have mastered the skills that the items represent. The skills and knowledge that teachers regard as *most important* tend to be the ones that those teachers stress in their instruction. And, even allowing for plenty of differences in teachers' instructional skills, the more that teachers stress certain content, the better their students will perform on items that measure such teacher-stressed content. But the better students perform on those items, the more likely it will be that those very items will be jettisoned when the standardized test is revised.

In short, the quest for score-spread creates a clearly identifiable tendency to remove from traditionally constructed standardized achievement tests those items that measure the most important, teacher-stressed content. Clearly, a test that deliberately dodges the most important things teachers try to teach should not be used to judge teachers' instructional success.

Items Linked to Test-Takers' Socioeconomic Status

Remember, the traditional measurement mission of standardized achievement tests is to provide accurate norm-referenced interpretations, and to do that, the test must produce ample score-spread. Again, due to limited test-administration time and the need to get maximum score variance from a minimal number of items, some of the items on standardized achievement tests are highly related to a student's socioeconomic status (SES).

Here's an example taken from a currently used standardized achievement test. It's a 6th grade science item, and I've modified it slightly, changing some words to preserve the test's security. I want to stress, though, that I have *not* altered the nature of the original item's *cognitive demand*—what it asks students to do.

AN SES-LINKED ITEM

Because a plant's fruit always contains seeds, which one of the following is not a fruit?
  a. pumpkin
  b. celery
  c. orange
  d. pear

If you look carefully at this sample item, you'll realize that children from more-privileged backgrounds (with parents who can routinely afford to buy fresh celery at the supermarket and purchase fresh pumpkins for Halloween carving) will generally do better on it than will children from less-privileged backgrounds (with parents who are eking out the family meals on government-issued food stamps). This is a classic SES-linked item.

It just so happens that socioeconomic status is a nicely spread-out variable, and it doesn't change all that rapidly. So, by linking test items to SES, the developers of standardized achievement tests are almost certain to get the score-spread they need. But *SES-linked items measure what students bring to school, not what they learn there.* For this reason, SES-linked items are not appropriate for evaluating instructional quality.

Items Linked to Test-Takers' Inherited Academic Aptitude

Children differ at birth, depending on what transpired during the gene-pool lottery. Some children are destined to grow up taller, heavier, or more attractive than their age-mates. Children also differ from birth in certain academic aptitudes, namely, in their verbal, quantitative, or spatial potentials.

From a teacher's perspective, classroom instruction would be far simpler if all children were born with *identical* academic aptitudes. But that's not the world we live in. We know, for example, that some children come into class with inherited quantitative smarts that exceed those of their classmates. Such children "catch on" quickly to most mathematical concepts, and they are likely to sail more easily through most of a school's mathematical challenges.

Of course, this is not to say that children born without superior quantitative aptitude should cease their mathematical journey shortly after mastering 2 + 2 or that they will not go on to high levels of mathematical prowess. It's just that children whose inborn quantitative aptitude is low will probably have to work harder and longer to do so. That's the way academic aptitudes work.

I concur with Howard Gardner's contention that there are *multiple intelligences*. Kids can be weak in verbal smarts, yet possess superb aesthetic smarts. I'm pretty good at mathematical stuff, yet I'm a blockhead when it comes to interpersonal sensitivities. Surely, there is not just one kind of intelligence. The people who create traditional standardized achievement tests are particularly concerned with three specific sorts: *quantitative*, *verbal*, and *spatial* aptitudes. You will find a good many items in standardized achievement tests that primarily assess these three kinds of smarts.

Consider, for example, the following 4th grade mathematics item. It, too, was drawn from a current standardized achievement test and is presented with only minor modifications to preserve test security.

AN INHERITED APTITUDE-LINKED ITEM

Which one of the letters below, when folded in half, can have exactly two matching parts?

a. Z

b. F

c. Y

d. S

Children who were born with ample spatial smarts will have a far easier time identifying the correct answer. (It's choice *c*.) Yes, this item is designed to measure a student's inborn spatial aptitude. It's certainly not measuring a skill that teachers promote through instruction. After all, how often is "mental letter-folding" taught in 4th grade mathematics classrooms? Answer: Never.

Like socioeconomic status, inherited academic aptitudes are nicely spread out in the population. By linking a test's items to one of these aptitudes, test developers have a better chance of creating the kind of score-spread that traditionally constructed standardized achievement tests must possess if they're going to carry out their comparative measurement mission properly.

But again: *inheritance-linked items measure what students bring to school, not what they learn there.* Such items are not appropriate for evaluating instructional quality. I suppose it could be argued that inheritance-linked items have a role to play in aptitude tests (especially if you regard such assessments as some sort of intelligence test). Still, aptitude-linked items really have no place at all in what is supposed to be an *achievement* test.

To reiterate, the measurement function of traditionally constructed standardized achievement tests is to permit relative comparisons among test-takers, usually by contrasting an individual's score with a norm-group's scores on the same test. For these relative (norm-referenced) comparisons to be accurate, the test must create a considerable spread in test-takers' scores. However, in the pursuit of score-spread, the developers of standardized achievement test often include items blatantly unsuitable for evaluating the effectiveness of instruction.

The Prevalence of Inappropriate Items

How many such score-spreading items are there in a typical standardized achievement test? Well, the number surely varies from test to test, but I recently went through a pair of different standardized achievement tests, item by item, at two different grade levels. I really was trying to be objective in my judgments, but if I thought the *dominant* factor in a student's coming up with a correct answer was either socioeconomic status or inherited academic aptitude, I flagged the item. These are the approximate percentages I found:

- 50 percent of reading items.
- 75 percent of language arts items.
- 15 percent of mathematics items.
- 85 percent of science items.
- 65 percent of social studies items.

Yes, it's a little shocking. Even if you were to cut my percentages in half (because, although I was trying to be objective, I may have let my biases blind me), these tests would still include way too many items that ought not to be used to evaluate the quality of instruction. But then, they are absolutely appropriate for a standardized test's traditional comparative assessment mission.

I challenge you to spend an hour or two with a copy of a standardized achievement test and do your own judging about the number of items in the test that careful analysis will reveal to be strongly dependent on children's socioeconomic status or on their inherited academic aptitudes. If you accept this challenge, let me caution against judging an item positively because you'd *like* a test-taker be able to answer the item correctly. Heck, we'd like *all* test-takers to answer *every* item correctly. Nor should you defer to the technical expertise of those who originally wrote the item. Remember, the item is apt to have been written to satisfy a different assessment function than the evaluation of educators' instructional effectiveness.

If you're up to this challenge, your task is to make a *Yes, No,* or *Uncertain* judgment about each test item based on this question:

> Will this test item, along with others, be helpful in determining what students were taught in school?

If your item-by-item scrutiny yields many *No* or *Uncertain* judgments because items are either SES-linked or inheritance-linked, then the test you're reviewing should definitely *not* be used to evaluate teachers' instructional success.

Another Problem: Standardized Tests' Ill-Defined Instructional Targets

With so much pressure on U.S. teachers to raise students' scores on standardized achievement tests, it is not surprising that a vigorous test-preparation industry has blossomed in this country. "Test-prep" booklets and computer programs now abound, and many are linked to a specific standardized achievement test. In some districts, teachers have been directed to devote substantial segments of their regular classroom time to unabashed preparation for a particular standardized achievement test, either a nationally published test or a test customized for their state's accountability program.

Unfortunately, because many of these state-customized tests were built by the same firms that distribute the national standardized achievement tests, they too have been developed according to the traditional score-spreading measurement model. As a consequence, these customized tests are often no better for evaluating instruction than an off-the-shelf, nationally standardized achievement test.

I realize that some of you reading this book may be teaching in states where a customized statewide test has been constructed so that it is closely aligned with the state's official content standards. Surely, you might think, the results of such a test must provide *some* insight into the quality of classroom instruction. Sadly, this is rarely the case.

One reason—a serious shortcoming of today's so-called standards-based tests and the whole standards-based reform strategy—is that these tests typically do not supply teachers with a report regarding a student's standard-by-standard mastery. How can teachers decide which aspects of their instruction need to be modified if they are unable to determine which content standards their students have mastered and which they have not? Without per-standard reporting, all that teachers get is a general and potentially misleading report of students' overall standards mastery. This information has little instructional value.

Another instructional shortcoming of most standards-based tests is that they don't spell out what they're actually measuring with sufficient clarity so that a teacher can teach toward the bodies of skills and knowledge the tests represent. Remember, a test is only supposed to represent (that is, *sample*) a body of knowledge and skills. Based on the student's score on that test-created representation, the teacher reaches an inference about the student's content mastery. But, as we discussed back in Chapter 2, the teacher should direct the actual instruction—and *all* test-preparation activities—toward the body of knowledge and skills represented by a specific set of test items, *not* toward the test itself. I've represented this graphically in Figure 9.1.

For purposes of a teacher's instructional decision making, the difficulty is that the description of what the standardized achievement test measures is typically way too skimpy to help a teacher direct instruction properly. Why then don't test developers just take the time to provide instructionally helpful descriptions? Well, remember that as long as a traditional standardized achievement test provides satisfactory comparative interpretations, there's no compelling reason for the developers to do so.

9.1 | **PROPER AND IMPROPER DIRECTIONS FOR A TEACHER'S INSTRUCTIONAL EFFORTS**

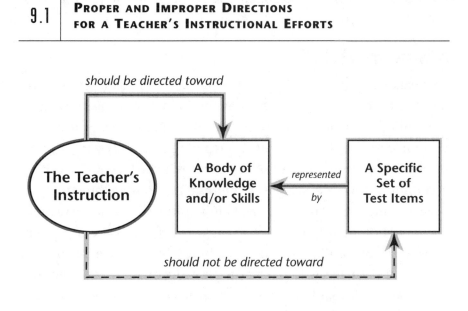

As you'll see in the next chapter, it is possible to create standardized achievement tests so they actually do define what they assess at a level suitable for instructional decision making. However, if you find yourself forced to use a traditional standardized achievement test, you must be wary of teaching too specifically toward the test's actual items. Your litmus test when judging your own test-preparation activities should be your answer to the following question:

> Will this test-preparation activity not only improve students' test performance, but also improve their mastery of the skills and knowledge this test represents?

Oh, it's all right to give students an hour or two of preparation dealing with *general test-taking tactics,* such as how to allocate test-taking time judiciously or how to make informed guesses. But beyond such brief one-size-fits-all preparation to help students cope with the trauma of test taking, your instruction should focus on what the test *represents*, not on the test itself.

A Misleading Label?

For years, educators have been using the label "standardized achievement tests" to identify tests such as the Iowa Tests of Basic Skills or the California Achievement Tests, and the term is in even greater circulation these days as each state is preparing to comply with the new measurement requirements of the No Child Left Behind Act. But according to my dictionary, *achievement* refers to something that has been accomplished "through great effort." In fact, that same dictionary describes an *achievement test* as "a test to measure a person's knowledge or proficiency in something that can be learned or taught." It's safe to say that *most* people think of an achievement test as a measure of what "students have learned in school," which is one reason so many educational policymakers automatically believe that students' scores on standardized achievement tests provide a defensible indication of a school's instructional quality.

What most people don't know, but you now do, is that the historic mission of standardized testing is at cross-purposes with the intent of achievement testing. And because of the historic need to produce score-spread, standardized achievement tests don't do a very good job of measuring what students have learned in school through their efforts and the efforts of their teachers. As I've indicated, a substantial part of a student's score on a standardized achievement test is likely to reflect not what was taught in school, but what the student brought to school in the first place.

Our educational community is, in my view, partially to blame for today's widespread misconception that standardized achievement tests can be used to determine instructional quality. (I fault myself, too, for I should personally have been working much harder to help dissuade both educators and the public from the idea that standardized test scores accurately reflect educational quality.) But it's not too late to start correcting this prevalent and harmful misconception.

I encourage you to spread the word, first among your colleagues and then to parents and other concerned citizens. There *are* legitimate ways to evaluate instructional quality, and we'll look at some of these in the next two chapters. But please do what you can to get the word out that evaluating instructional quality with traditional standardized achievement tests is flat-out wrong.

INSTRUCTIONALLY FOCUSED TESTING TIPS

• Explain to colleagues and parents why standardized achievement tests' traditional function to provide accurate norm-referenced interpretations is dependent on sufficient score-spread among students' test performances.

• Describe to colleagues and parents how it is that three types of score-spreading items (mid-difficulty items, SES-linked items, and aptitude-linked items) reduce the suitability of traditionally constructed standardized achievement tests for evaluating instructional quality.

• Spend time reviewing an actual standardized achievement test's items to determine the proportion of items you regard as unsuitable for determining what students were taught in school.

• Recognize that the descriptive information supplied with traditional standardized achievement tests does not describe the skills and knowledge represented by those tests in a manner adequate to support teachers' instructional decision making.

Recommended Resources

Cizek, G. J. (1999). *Cheating on tests: How to do it, detect it, and prevent it.* Mahwah, NJ: Lawrence Erlbaum Associates.

Kohn, A. (2000). *The case against standardized testing: Raising the scores, ruining the schools.* Westport, CT: Heinemann.

Kohn, A. (Program Consultant). (2000). *Beyond the standards movement: Defending quality education in an age of test scores* [Videotape]. Port Chester, NY: National Professional Resources, Inc.

Lemann, N. (2002). *The big test: The secret history of the American meritocracy.* New York: Farrar, Straus and Giroux.

Northwest Regional Educational Laboratory. (1991). *Understanding standardized tests* [Videotape]. Los Angeles: IOX Assessment Associates.

Popham, W. J. (Program Consultant). (2000). *Standardized achievement tests: Not to be used in judging school quality* [Videotape]. Los Angeles: IOX Assessment Associates.

Popham, W. J. (Program Consultant). (2002). *Evaluating schools: Right tasks, wrong tests* [Videotape]. Los Angeles: IOX Assessment Associates.

Sacks, P. (1999). *Standardized minds: The high price of America's testing culture and what we can do to change it.* Cambridge, MA: Perseus Books.

Instructionally Supportive Standards-Based Tests

IN THIS CHAPTER AND THE NEXT, I'LL BE CONSIDERING ONE OF THE MOST SIG-
nificant links between instruction and assessment: the role that test
results can play in the evaluation of a teacher's instructional effectiveness. In the previous chapter, you saw why the results of traditionally constructed standardized achievement tests should never be
used to judge teachers' instructional effectiveness. Well, if those tests
aren't the answer, what is?

Making the Best of the Situation . . .
and Seeking the Best for the Students

Some educators long for a return to those tranquil days of yesteryear
when there were no educational accountability programs and no
annual achievement tests with results employed to evaluate educators. In my view, that sort of yearning is a definite no-yield yearn.
Instead of resisting today's test-based evaluative pressures, we ought
to be redirecting those pressures into processes that help children
receive a better education.

Let's be realistic. Educational accountability programs aren't going
to evaporate in the near or distant future. The public has serious

doubts about whether educators are doing an adequate job of teaching the nation's children. What's more, people want hard evidence, not verbal reassurance, that classroom teachers are delivering high-quality instruction. And the evidence forming the core of all educational accountability programs will continue to be students' performance on tests that measure mastery of important skills and knowledge. Moreover, those tests will be *standardized* to prevent educators from collecting evidence via a set of possibly suspect "home-grown" tests. No, the public wants credible, test-based evidence of what students have learned in school. Fine! Let's supply them with that kind of evidence. But let's do it in a way that helps teachers to help students.

Standards-Based Achievement Tests

Many states now evaluate public school students through custom-built statewide tests, administered each year. Typically, these tests are constructed to be aligned with a state's curricular goals (its set of official content standards). Accordingly, these statewide standardized achievement tests are usually referred to as *standards-based tests*.

As I've noted, many of these tests have (sadly) been constructed in precisely the same way that traditional standardized achievement tests are built, with the result that they are similarly score-spread focused and thus unsuitable for evaluating educational quality. What's more, these customized, standards-based achievement tests offer no more instructional benefits to teachers than traditional standardized tests do. What we need are *untraditional* standardized achievement tests—ones that do not rely on norm-referenced comparisons but that still provide the evaluative evidence that the architects of educational accountability programs demand. The trick, then, is to install standardized tests that do a decent accountability job but also help teachers do a better job of instructing students. This can be done.

What Makes a Standards-Based Achievement Test Instructionally Supportive?

Before we look at the three features that an accountability focused standardized test must have in order to help teachers boost instruction, I need to explain how to distinguish between tests that yield *norm-referenced* interpretations and tests that yield *criterion-referenced* interpretations.

As you read in the previous chapter, when a test's results allow a student's score to be "referenced" back to the scores of a norm group, we call this a *norm-referenced interpretation* or a *norm-referenced inference*. If a test's results allow us to "reference" a student's score back to a clearly defined skill or body of knowledge, this is called a *criterion-referenced interpretation* or a *criterion-referenced inference*. A norm-referenced interpretation might be something like this: "Jamal scored at the 93rd percentile on the standardized achievement test." A criterion-referenced interpretation might be "Hillary's test score indicated she had mastered 85 percent of the 500 words in the 'spelling demons' word list."

Please note that it is not *a test* that is norm-referenced or criterion-referenced, but the score-based *inference*. Indeed, a test can be specifically built to provide both norm- and criterion-referenced interpretations. What people usually mean when they talk about a "norm-referenced test" is that the test is built so it typically yields norm-referenced inferences about test-takers.

Well, the kind of instructionally supportive standardized achievement test educators need to both boost instructional quality and supply accountability evidence must be constructed to provide meaningful *criterion-referenced* interpretations. This is essential, because it means that test developers are off the hook when it comes to score-spread. If no one is interested in comparing test-takers with the norm group, then it's no longer necessary to include the score-spreading items. What the test-makers must do, however, is create a standardized achievement test that will provide reasonably accurate evidence about children's mastery of *particular* content standards. And that brings us to the first characteristic of an instructionally supportive standardized achievement test.

Standard-by-Standard Reporting

An instructionally supportive standardized achievement test must provide standard-by-standard results for each student who is tested. If teachers have this kind of per-standard information for individual students, they can correlate the achievement test's results with what they already know about particular students' strengths and weaknesses. They can then use this combined information to reconsider the merits of their instructional approaches. For instance: "James, Sarita, Bisham, and Jack all struggle with mathematics. They all scored well on Math Standards 1, 2, and 4, where I used Instructional Approach *A*; they all scored poorly on Standard 3, where I did not. Perhaps next year, I should try to employ Instructional Approach *A* with Standard 3." Unless teachers discover which content standards have or haven't been mastered by students, they cannot know which elements of their instruction to retain and which to retool.

Currently, few states' standards-based tests yield per-standard results for students. And yet, these statewide tests supposedly serve as the cornerstones of a "standards-based reform" strategy intended to improve a state's public education. What teachers in most states are given, after each year's tests have been scored, is some sort of global report indicating how a *group* of students have done *generally* with respect to the state's *total array* of official content standards. A statewide test might provide teachers with the following sort of report: "Based on our state's mathematics test, on the 6 content standards related to *statistics,* 37 percent of your students scored at the *advanced* level, 23 percent scored at the *proficient* level, 24 percent scored at the *basic* level, and 16 percent scored at the *below basic* level." Is it any wonder that teachers do not regard such standards-based tests as instructionally helpful?

Standard-by-standard reporting would not only benefit teachers, but also parents, who would receive specific information about their child's mastery of key content standards. And, of course, there are the students themselves. Wouldn't *your* students benefit if they could each discover which standards they had mastered? Standard-by-standard reporting is indispensable if a standards-based test is going to make a genuine contribution to improved instruction.

Accurate Assessment of Only the Highest Priority Content Standards

The second characteristic of an instructionally supportive standards-based test proceeds necessarily from the first. If a standards-based test is to supply standard-by-standard results, it must contain a sufficient number of items per content standard to allow for accurate inferences about students' per-standard mastery. However, allowing for more items per content standard will mean that tests will be able to assess fewer standards overall.

Presumably, then, an instructionally supportive standards-based test that must be administered within a two-hour period might well end up assessing only a half-dozen or so content standards. It is therefore critical that all of the assessed standards be truly significant. This will require the architects of standards-based tests to prioritize their state's official content standards so that every test form always assesses the *most important* standards. From an instructional perspective, it is better for tests to measure a handful of powerful skills accurately than it is for tests to do an inaccurate job of measuring many skills.

Ideally, the standards at the top of the test-developers' prioritized list will be those that embody significant cognitive skills that subsume lesser subskills and bodies of knowledge. A good example of such a powerful skill is students' ability to compose original essays of various types—persuasive essays, for example. When educators assess students' mastery of this skill by having students create writing samples, those samples can be evaluated overall (using holistic rubrics) and with respect to a variety of subskills such as organization and mechanics (using analytic rubrics).

And students' mastery of these high-import skills can definitely be used in educational accountability programs to help evaluate schools or districts. For example, suppose that students' performances on a writing-skills test had been categorized as *advanced, proficient, basic,* and *below basic.* It would be quite straightforward to calculate the percentages of a district's students who scored in each of those four performance levels, then compare districts on that basis. (Indeed, the No Child Left Behind Act requires schools, districts, and states to set at least *basic, proficient,* and *advanced* performance standards and demonstrate yearly increases in the proportion of students deemed proficient or above. It's easy to imagine comparisons based on these data.) In short, the kinds of tests I'm describing here would help teachers teach better and *still* produce the evidence necessary to make accountability programs function in the long-term best interests of children.

The major drawback to the per-standard assessment of high-priority content standards is the risk that pervasive pressure to improve students' test performances will lead schools to give too little instructional attention to lower-priority content standards *not* assessed on the statewide standards-based test. This kind of narrowing of what's taught will inevitably short-change our students.

To counter such tendencies toward curricular reductionism, teachers should demand that district or state authorities provide an array of optional classroom assessment instruments. Such instruments could be used to measure students' mastery of those state-approved content standards that, although worthwhile for children to master, are not assessed by a statewide standards-based test. In addition, educators at the school, district, and state levels should come up with ways of monitoring curricular breadth so that those content standards (and those subject areas) not assessed on a statewide test will still receive instructional and assessment attention in the state's classrooms.

Clear Assessment Descriptions for Each Measured Content Standard

Finally, the skills and knowledge being assessed by an instructionally supportive standards-based test must be described well enough so that teachers truly understand what they must teach to promote mastery. Therefore, each of the high-priority content standards assessed must be accompanied by an *assessment description* that sets forth, in two or three teacher-friendly paragraphs, just what a student needs to be able to do cognitively to perform well on the items measuring a particular content standard. These brief assessment descriptions would clarify for teachers what sorts of cognitive demands a given content standard's items will impose on students. Several illustrative, but nonexhaustive sample items should accompany each assessment description. Necessarily, all samples for a particular content standard would impose the same cognitive demand. Ideally, they should be different item-types, to promote generalizable mastery.

The availability of assessment descriptions for each assessed content standard would make it possible for teachers to aim their instruction toward students' mastery of the skills and knowledge *represented* by a standards-based test, not toward the test itself. And that, we know, is just how the instruction game is supposed to be played. If teachers aim their instruction only at a set of particular test items, then *test-scores* may improve, but students' *mastery* of what the test represents surely won't.

To review, then, the three key features of instructionally supportive accountability tests* are (1) *standard-by-standard reporting,* (2) *accurate assessment of only the highest priority content standards,* and (3) *clear assessment description for each measured content standard.*

---

*For a more detailed consideration of how instructionally supportive accountability tests can be constructed, see the October 2001 report of the Commission on Instructionally Supportive Assessment, *Building Tests That Support Instruction and Accountability: A Guide for Policymakers.* Available online at www.aasa.org, www.naesp.org, www.principals.org, www.nea.org, and www.nmsa.org.

What Could Be

To give you an idea of what a statewide accountability test might look like if it were constructed along the instructionally useful lines I recommend, I've provided a brief illustration in Figure 10.1.

The accountability-focused testing program described in the figure is fictional, but there's no reason that it couldn't be a reality. I hope I've convinced you that it *is* possible to create high-stakes, statewide tests that not only provide credible accountability evidence, but also help teachers do a better job of instructing their students.

So what can you, a teacher, do to make sure your schools use instructionally supportive tests for their accountability programs? Well, you can exert whatever influence you have, perhaps through your professional association, to see that such tests are made available. Educational policymakers at every level must first be educated about these assessment issues, then urged to endorse the use of instructionally supportive standards-based tests.

If you prefer a less activist role, then set out to do a solid job of educating your own colleagues about why it is that traditional standardized achievement tests ought not be used to evaluate schools. Then let your colleagues know why it is that instructionally supportive tests should be used for that purpose. And don't forget to pass on information about these issues to your students' parents. Parents of school-age children have a major stake in seeing that the standardized tests used with their children will help, not harm, the instruction those children receive.

SAMPLE DESCRIPTION OF A STATE-LEVEL, INSTRUCTIONALLY SUPPORTIVE ACCOUNTABILITY TESTING PROGRAM

Overview. *State X*'s accountability tests, administered annually in grades 3–8 and grade 10, each assess the state's most significant content standards.

Content assessed. The state has identified approximately 100 content standards in every subject that is assessed. However, committees of state educators and non-educator citizens have prioritized those content standards so that each grade level's accountability test assesses between five and nine of the highest-priority standards. The state's curriculum authorities made a serious effort to devise a defensible grade-to-grade articulation for each content standard across the grade levels tested.

Assessment descriptions. Every state-assessed content standard's key elements are spelled out in brief, state-published assessment descriptions that most teachers rely on when devising their instructional plans.

Results reporting. Because the accountability tests provide annual reports regarding each student's standard-by-standard achievement levels, the state's teachers can readily determine which parts of their standards-focused instruction are working and which parts are not. Students and their parents also receive annual reports regarding each student's mastery of every state-assessed content standard.

Test-focused professional development. The state's teachers and administrators are routinely provided with professional development programs related directly to the statewide accountability program. One theme of these programs addresses the best ways for teachers to improve their instruction based on analyses of their students' per-standard test performances. A second professional-development theme deals with how teachers can construct their own classroom assessments to measure those state-approved content standards that, although important for children to master, cannot be accurately measured in the time that is available for state-level testing.

Sample assessments. This year, for the first time, state authorities have distributed an optional set of classroom assessments designed to measure students' mastery of the state-assessed content standards for each grade level tested. Teachers are encouraged to use these optional assessments during the school year in a formative evaluative fashion, that is, to determine how students are progressing toward mastery of the state-assessed content standards.

Measures to assure curricular breadth. State officials have described several procedures for monitoring a school's curricular breadth. The state requires each school's staff to use one of those monitoring mechanisms annually to supply evidence regarding the richness of the curricular targets addressed instructionally in that school's classrooms. State officials have also made available to teachers a substantial number of optional classroom assessments that teachers can employ to measure their students' mastery of "state-approved but state-*unassessed*" content standards.

Summation. Although the state's districts and schools are rigorously evaluated each year on the basis of the accountability tests' results as well as other evidence (such as teachers' pretest/post-test data and students' attendance rates), the state's teachers appear to be reasonably well satisfied with the accountability program because, given their understanding of what is to be promoted instructionally, most teachers have assembled evidence that they are doing a solid job of teaching. Based on students' assessed progress in mastering the state-tested content standards, the state's teachers appear to be successful.

INSTRUCTIONALLY FOCUSED TESTING TIPS

• Inform your colleagues about the attributes of standards-based tests that make such tests instructionally supportive: standard-by-standard reporting, accurate assessment of only the highest priority content standards, and clear assessment descriptions for each measured content standard.

• Influence policymakers to replace, or at least supplement, traditionally constructed standardized achievement tests with instructionally supportive standards-based tests.

Recommended Resources

Commission on Instructionally Supportive Assessment. *Building tests to support instruction and accountability: A guide for policymakers.* Washington, DC: Author.

Kiernan, L. J. (Producer). (1996). *Reporting student progress* [Videotape]. Alexandria, VA: Association for Supervision and Curriculum Development.

Linn, R. L. (2000, March). Assessments and accountability. *Educational Researcher, 29*(2), 4–16.

Popham, W. J. (2001). *The truth about testing: An educator's call to action:* Alexandria, VA: Association for Supervision and Curriculum Development.

Collecting Credible Classroom Evidence of Instructional Impact

As I've noted, the chief reason that the designers of educational accountability systems rely on standardized tests is that those designers don't trust educators to provide truly accurate evidence regarding their own classroom successes or failures. And let's be honest: That's not an absurd reason for incredulity. No one really likes to be evaluated and found wanting. The architects of educational accountability systems typically make students' standardized test scores the centerpiece of their evaluative activities because it's accepted that such tests provide more believable evidence.

However, because no *single* source of data should ever be employed to make significant decisions about schools, teachers, or students, even standardized test scores should be supplemented by other evidence of teachers' instructional success. This supplemental evidence of a teacher's instructional impact must clearly be *credible*. If evidence of effective instruction is not truly credible, well, no one will believe it . . . and it won't do any good.

A Post-Test–Focused Data-Gathering Design

You'll recall from Chapter 1 that one of the major drawbacks of using data from a once-a-year standardized achievement test (even an instructionally supportive one) to see how well a teacher has taught is that the quality of students in a given teacher's class varies from year to year. If a 5th grade teacher's class this year is brimming with bright, motivated children, those students are apt to perform pretty well on this year's standardized test. But if a year later, the same teacher draws a markedly less able collection of 5th graders, the students' test scores are apt to be much lower. Does this year-to-year drop in 5th graders' scores indicate that the teacher's instructional effectiveness had decreased? Of course not. *The students were different.*

The key to getting a more accurate fix on a teacher's true instructional impact is to collect evidence from the *same* students while they remain with the *same* teacher. One way to do this, represented in Figure 11.1, is to test the teacher's students after instruction is finished. This is called a *post-test–only* design and its chief weakness—for teachers who would employ it—is that it doesn't factor in the students' pre-instruction status. If your students score superbly on the post-instruction test, is it because you taught them well or because the tested material was something they all learned years ago? With no basis for comparison, the post-test–only design flops if you're trying to isolate the impact of your instruction.

11.1 | **A POST-TEST–ONLY DATA-GATHERING DESIGN**

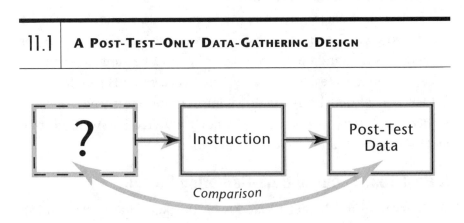

The Pretest/Post-Test Data-Gathering Design

The most common data-gathering model teachers use to get a picture of how well they have taught their students is a straightforward *pretest/post-test model* such as the one presented graphically in Figure 11.2. (You also saw this data-gathering model in Chapter 1.) Most of us are familiar with how this works: a teacher gives students the same test, once before instruction and again after. Elementary teachers, for example, might administer a 20-item test at the start of a school year and the same test again at year's end. Secondary teachers in schools on a semester system might administer a test at the semester's outset and then again at its conclusion.

11.2 | **A PRETEST/POST-TEST DATA-GATHERING DESIGN**

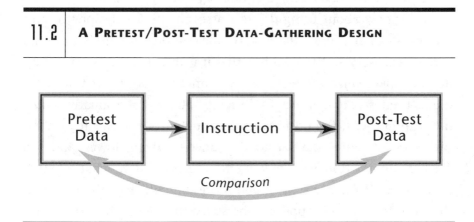

The virtue of the classic pretest/post test evaluative model is that, for the most part, it does measure the same group of students before instruction and after, meaning that a comparative analysis of the two sets of test data provides a clearer picture of the teacher's instructional impact on student mastery levels than do post-test data alone. In classrooms with high student mobility, it is usually sensible to compare pretest and post-test performances of only those students who have been in the class long enough for the relevant instruction to "work." Thus, whereas all students might take a post-instruction assessment, for purposes of appraising instructional effectiveness, you would *analyze* the post-test scores of just the students who had been enrolled in the class for, say, eight weeks or whatever instructional period seems sufficient.

There are problems with the pretest/post-test model that reduces its accuracy. One major drawback that occurs when a teacher uses the same test before and after instruction is referred to as *pretest reactivity*. What this means is that students' experience taking a pretest will often make them react differently to the post-test. They have been sensitized to "what's coming." A skeptic might conclude that even if post-test scores went up, students didn't necessary learn anything; perhaps they simply figured out how to take the test the second time through. Unfortunately, the skeptic might be right.

Well, how about using *different* assessments for the pretest and the post-test? It sounds like a good idea, and it definitely prevents pretest reactivity, but the truth is that it is much more difficult than most people realize to create two genuinely equidifficult tests. And unless the tests are identical in difficulty, all sorts of evaluative craziness can ensue. If the post-test is the tougher of the two tests, then the post-test scores have a good chance of being lower, and the teacher's instruction will look ineffective no matter what. On the other hand, if the pretest is much more difficult than the post-test, then the teacher will appear to be successful even when that's not true. No, there are definite difficulties associated with a teacher's use of the rudimentary kind of pretest/post-test model seen in Figure 11.2. But this model can be improved.

A Better Source of Evidence: The Split-and-Switch Data-Gathering Design

Let me describe a way to collect instruction data for a pretest versus post-test comparison that skirts the difficulties associated with the standard pretest/post-test design. I call it the *split-and-switch* model, and here's how to use it in your classroom.

▲ **Choose a skill.** Select an important skill that your students should acquire as a consequence of your instruction over a substantial period of time (a semester or school year). The more important the skill being taught and tested, the more impressive will be any evidence of your instructional impact.

▲ **Choose your assessment type.** I recommend you opt for a constructed-response test, which is almost always the best choice to assess important skills. Performance tests are often ideal. Don't forget, though, that if you choose a constructed-response format, you'll also need to design a rubric to evaluate students' responses.

▲ **Create two assessments.** Now, instead of designing one assessment to measure your students' mastery of the skill, design *two*—two versions that measure the same variable. Let's call them *Form A* and *Form B*. The two forms should require approximately the same administration time and, although they should be similar in difficulty, they need not be identical in difficulty.

▲ **Create two test groups.** Randomly divide your class into two halves. You could simply use your alphabetical class list and split the class into two half-classes: A–L last names and M–Z last names. Let's call these *Half-Class 1* and *Half-Class 2*.

▲ **Pretest, teach, and post-test.** Finally, you'll come to the testing. As a *pretest,* administer one test form to one test group, and the other test form to the other test group (for example, Half-Class 1 takes Form A and Half-Class 2 takes Form B). As you might have already guessed, at the end of instruction, you will *post-test* by switching the two test forms so that each test group gets the test form it didn't get at pretest time.

▲ **Compare data sets.** You'll end up with two sets of comparative data to consider: the Form A pretests versus the Form A post-tests and the Form B pretests versus the Form B post-tests. The split-and-switch design is depicted graphically in Figure 11.3, where you can see the two appropriate comparisons to make.

11.3 | THE SPLIT-AND-SWITCH DATA-GATHERING DESIGN

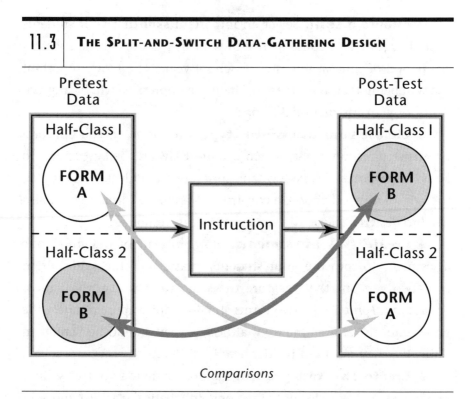

Comparisons

What you want to see, of course, are results indicating that the vast majority of high test performances were produced at post-test time. There will be no pretest reactivity because each half-class gets what is to them a brand new test form as a post-test. And because this data-gathering design yields *two* separate indications of a teacher's instructional impact, the results (positive or negative) ought to confirm one another. Remember, even if Form A is very tough and Form B is not, you're comparing the tough Form A pretests with the tough Form A post-tests, and the easy Form B post-tests with the easy Form B post-tests.

Credibility-Enhancing Measures

Now, although you could use this model as is, without any refinements, I don't think you should. Here's what I recommend.

▲ **"Blind score" the pretests and post-tests.** The rationale behind blind scoring is to counteract every teacher's understandable desire to see improvement even if it may not be in evidence. When creating your two test forms, also create identical response-booklets that you'll pass out to all students, both at pretest and post-test time. Tell students not to put dates on their response booklets. When you collect the completed response booklets at pretest time, code them on the reverse side of the last sheet so that it's possible, but not easy, to tell that the responses are pretests. You might use a short string of numbers, and make the second number an odd number (1, 3, 5, 7, or 9). Go ahead and look at your students' pretest responses if you'd like to get an idea of your students' skill levels at the beginning of instruction, but do not make any marks on their test forms. File the forms away.

At the end of the semester or school year, conduct a similar coding procedure when you collect the post-tests, but make the second number in your code string an even number. Again, you can use these post-tests as you would any other (to make inferences about what your students have learned), but if you use post-tests for grading purposes, be sure to take into consideration any difficulty-level differences you may have detected between Form A and Form B.

Finally, when it comes time to compare the two sets of data, mix all the Form A responses together (Form A pretests and post-tests). Do the same for the Form B responses. After you've scored them, use the codes to separate out your pretests and post-tests, and then see what the data have to say about your instructional effectiveness.

▲ **Bring in nonpartisan judges.** You can enhance the credibility of your evidence even further by turning over pretest/post-test evaluations to someone else, thereby ensuring undistorted judgment. (If you've spent some time with your students' pretests to help you determine entry-level skills or with the post-tests for grading purposes, you'll probably recognize which are which, despite your best efforts.)

Parent volunteers make great nonpartisan blind-scorers. Provide them with an evaluation rubric and a brief orientation to its use. The judges will get all the Form A responses (both pretests and post-tests thoroughly mixed together) and then score the responses. *After* all the Form A responses have been scored and returned to you, use your coding system to sort the responses into pretests and post-tests. Then, it's just a matter of comparing your students' pretest responses with their post-test responses. Use the same process for blind-scoring the Form B tests.

If you've used nonpartisan judges and they have blind-scored your students' papers properly, the results ought to be truly credible to the accountability minded. The results should help you, and the external world, know if your instruction is working.

Caveats for Using the Model

Of course, even the best-laid evaluative schemes can be foiled. The major weakness in the split-and-switch model is that some teachers might teach toward the test forms themselves, thereby eroding the validity of any test-based inferences about students' true skill mastery. Always teach only toward the *skill* being promoted; never teach toward the tests being used to measure skill mastery.

Another potential problem is that, in order to produce stable data, the split-and-switch model requires a relatively large group of students. A class of around 30 is ideal. If your class is much smaller (say, 20 students or less), it's best to revert to a standard pretest/post-test model, even with its drawbacks. You can still employ the kind of nonpartisan blind-scoring process I've described, which will increase the likelihood of your pretest/post-test data being regarded as credible.

Though not flawless, the split-and-switch design can help you buttress the evidence of your instructional effectiveness in a more believable manner. And, of course, if this test-based evidence suggests that your instruction isn't working as well as you wish, you will need to address that shortcoming through the use of alternative instructional strategies.

I urge you to consider employing a split-and-switch design to evaluate your effectiveness in promoting your students' mastery of a very limited number of high-import outcomes. Let's be honest. Implementation of this data-gathering design takes time and is clearly more trouble than conventional testing. Use it judiciously, but do use it. I think you'll like it.

Comparisons of "Pre-" and "Post-" Affective Data

Pretest/post-test contrasts of students' attitudes, interests, or values as measured on self-report inventories are a final source of useful credible evidence regarding a teacher's own instructional effectiveness.

Remember, if you will, the confidence inventories described in Chapter 8 and the positive relations between students' expressed confidence in being able to use a skill and their actual possession of that skill. If you can assemble pretest/post-test evidence, collected anonymously, indicating that your students' confidence has grown appreciably with respect to their ability to perform significant cognitive skills, these results will reflect very favorably on your instruction.

If you do decide to collect pretest/post-test affective evidence as an indication of your own instructional success, remember that you need to collect it in a manner that even nonbelievers will regard as credible. Just spend a few mental moments, casting yourself in the role of a doubter. Pretend you are a person who has serious doubts about whether the evidence you'll be presenting about your own instructional effectiveness is believable. Do whatever you can, in the collection of any evaluative evidence, to allay the concerns that such a doubter might have. Happily, a split-and-switch design, especially if students' responses are blind-scored by nonpartisans, will take care of most of a disbeliever's concerns.

If you are worried about pretest reactivity—and such reactivity often is a concern when assessing affect—you can employ a split-and-switch design, simply chopping your affective inventories into two half-inventories so that students will get different inventories as pretests and post-tests.

Final Thoughts

There are a number of ways that properly constructed educational tests can contribute to the quality of a teacher's instructional decisions. In my opinion, however, there is no more important contribution than helping a teacher supply an answer to the question "How effective was my instruction?"

There are also a number of ways to judge a teacher's success. Many factors ought to be considered, some of which are not test-based in any way. We can gain insights into a school staff's effectiveness by considering the school's statistics regarding truancy, tardiness, and dropouts. At the secondary school level, we can look at how many students decide to pursue postsecondary education. And surely, any sort of sensible teacher-evaluation model must consider a teacher's classroom conduct.

Few would argue, however, the most important evidence regarding instructional effectiveness must revolve around *what students learn*. And tests can help teachers by allowing them not only to determine for themselves what students have learned, but also to tell that story to the world. In this chapter, two test-based sources of evaluative evidence were considered: pretest/post-test cognitive assessments and pretest/post-test affective assessments. The evidence you can collect from both of those approaches, ideally buttressing your students' performances on the kinds of instructionally supportive standards-based tests described in Chapter 10, will provide you with a defensible notion of how well you've been teaching. If the use of those kinds of evidence can help you decide which parts of your instruction are working and which parts aren't, then you can keep the winning parts and overhaul the losing parts. Your students deserve no less.

INSTRUCTIONALLY FOCUSED TESTING TIPS

- Collect truly credible pretest/post-test evidence of instructional impact regarding students' mastery of important cognitive skills.
- Use the split-and-switch design judiciously in your own classes, applying it only to the pretest/post-test appraisal of a limited number of high-import outcomes.
- Use pretest/post-test affective inventories to determine students' affective changes.

Recommended Resources

Bridges, E. M., & Groves, B. R. (2000). The macro- and micropolitics of personnel evaluation: A framework. *Journal of Personnel Evaluation in Education, 13*(4), 321–337.

Guskey, T., & Johnson, D. (Presenters). (1996). Alternative ways to document and communicate student learning [Audiotape]. Alexandria, VA: Association for Supervision and Curriculum Development.

Popham, W. J. (Program Consultant). (2000). *Evidence of school quality: How to collect it!* [Videotape]. Los Angeles: IOX Assessment Associates.

Popham, W. J. (2001). *The truth about testing: An educator's call to action.* Alexandria, VA: Association for Supervision and Curriculum Development.

Popham, W. J. (Program Consultant). (2002). *How to evaluate schools* [Videotape]. Los Angeles: IOX Assessment Associates.

Shepard, L. (2000, October). The role of assessment in a learning culture. *Educational Researcher, 29*(7), 4–14.

Stiggins, R. J. (2001). *Student-involved classroom assessment* (4th ed.). Upper Saddle River, NJ: Prentice Hall.

Stiggins, R. J., & Davies, A. (Program Consultants). (1996). *Student-involved conferences: A professional development video* [Videotape]. Portland, OR: Assessment Training Institute.

Cora in Her Classroom: An Illustration of Instructionally Focused Testing

I WANT TO WRAP UP THIS BOOK BY ILLUSTRATING SOME OF THE WAYS THAT A classroom teacher might employ my strategies for using tests to inform, improve, and evaluate classroom instruction. This excursion into make-believe focuses on Cora Clark, an imaginary but alliteratively named educator who teaches four classes of 9th grade English in an urban middle school.

State-Sanctioned Content Standards

In the state where Cora teaches, there are state board of education–endorsed content standards for all major subjects in grades K–12. Moreover, there are statewide exams that are administered each spring to all students in grades 3–10. The exams are supposed to measure students' mastery of the board-endorsed content standards.

Cora has consulted the list of approved content standards, and she has identified five broad content standards that appear to be particularly applicable to her middle school English classes. Moreover, beneath *each* of those content standards, there are from two to six "grade-level benchmarks" that identify the particular grade-level skills and knowledge that students should master. Most of these grade-level benchmarks are accompanied by one or two sample test items illustrating how the state intends to assess students' mastery of those benchmarks.

Although the state's verbal descriptions of these benchmarks are far less clear than Cora would prefer, the sample items do help her get a better idea of what the benchmarks really mean. In fact, Cora routinely looks *first* at a benchmark's sample items to try to figure out what each item assesses. Only afterward does she consult the language employed to describe a grade-level benchmark. As Cora tells other members of her school's faculty, "The real proof of our state's muddled benchmark-puddings always comes down to how each benchmark is actually going to be measured."

One of Cora's five "most important" content standards is "Appropriate Oral Communication." That standard lists two benchmarks for 9th graders, and the first is "students will be able to deliver effective oral reports to their classmates." Cora knows that in her district's high schools, most teachers expect students to be able to make oral presentations to their classmates. In truth, Cora believes mastery of oral presentations is necessary for her students' success in *life*—not just their success in high school. She regards this benchmark, and the oral communication content it represents, as altogether sensible curricular aims.

A State-Unassessed Skill

As Cora reads through the state-issued descriptive information about content standards and benchmarks, she notices that neither of the grade-level benchmarks underlying the "Appropriate Oral Communication" content standard will be measured on the state's annual spring tests. Cora assumes that the state's reluctance to assess students' oral communication skills is based, at least in part, on the practical difficulties of assessing that sort of oral skill on a large-scale basis. Nevertheless, she regards these skills as sufficiently important to promote actively in all four of her 9th grade classes.

Because she has no state-provided sample items to illustrate this state-unassessed content standard, Cora needs to decide for herself how she will determine student mastery. For the first benchmark, Cora concludes that she will be satisfied that students have achieved this curricular aim if they can confidently deliver brief oral reports to the rest of the class. Thus, she *operationalizes* this particular benchmark by tying its attainment to her students' effective oral presentations to their classmates.

An Assessment-Triggered Task Analysis

Cora recognizes that for *instructional* purposes, she must understand more clearly what is really involved in attaining this benchmark. So she asks herself, "What is it that my students must know and be able to do in order to deliver effective oral reports to their classmates?"

She comes up with a brainstorm-generated task analysis that isolates a list of specific skills and subskills characterizing the cognitive demands placed on students when they make oral presentations. Cora concludes that students ought to

- Demonstrate familiarity with the topic.
- Organize a presentation into main points and subpoints.
- Consider audience interests and concerns.
- Incorporate vivid detail.
- Speak *to* audience members, not at them.
- Speak distinctly enough to be understood and maintain a steady speaking voice throughout the presentation.
- Understand that people process the information they hear differently than they process the information they see, and use techniques such as repetition and visual aids to address these differences.
- Be familiar with various techniques for calming public speaking nerves, such as visualization and breathing exercises.

Looking back at this list, Cora is rather pleased with its breadth. She realizes, of course, that she will be obliged to *teach* these skills and knowledge to her students if they are going to be able to master this important benchmark. She concludes that if students can make suitable extemporaneous speeches on fairly familiar topics with an overnight preparation period, the chances are very good that they'll be able to deliver effective oral reports about topics that they have become very familiar with through research. Accordingly, she decides to measure students' mastery of this key benchmark via their delivery of five-minute extemporaneous speeches to their classmates.

Cora also has an idea about how she'll track her students' progress toward the oral communication standard. Because her husband is a professed "video junkie," she has access to a high-quality video camera, fairly decent editing equipment, and a spouse who can operate both. She decides to pretest and post-test her students (in all four classes) at the beginning and end of the school year. She generates a set of a dozen speech topics that are likely to appeal to her students, such as "TV for Teens: Why We Watch What We Watch" and "Getting Along with Other Students in Middle School."

Although Cora could simply pretest, then post-test, her students, she decides to evaluate this aspect of her instruction (namely, the instruction focused on oral communication) more rigorously. Her husband's willingness to help her with the burdensome videotaping aspects of this project is a major factor in her decision to take it on. During the last few years, Cora has learned to carefully consider the amount of time and effort any particular testing approach will require before she uses it. She wants to make sure that she doesn't spend all her time—or all her students' time—in testing, preparing for tests, or scoring tests.

A Skill-Focused Rubric

At the same time that Cora creates the speech topics, she also devises a skill-focused rubric that she will use to evaluate her students' oral presentations. She isolates a small number of evaluative criteria to incorporate in the rubric (settling on three) and gives each of those criteria a short descriptive name. Her plan is to make these three criteria the basis for the instructional activities that will promote students' mastery of oral presentations.

Once she has a near-final version of the rubric, Cora asks two other English teachers in her school to critique her draft. They have few substantive criticisms, but do urge her to explain more completely what each of the rubric's evaluative criteria mean.

The rubric Cora has devised for this oral communication skill is based on the following three evaluative criteria: (1) *content*, that is, the substance of the presentation; (2) *organization*, that is, the structure of the presentation; and (3) *presentation*, that is, delivery procedures such as good eye contact, appropriate voice control, and the avoidance of distracting mannerisms. Taking the advice of her colleagues, Cora creates—and supplies to her students—a brief written explanation of each criterion's meaning.

As the year progresses, these three criteria dominate *all* of Cora's instruction related to oral presentations. It's Cora's hope that her students will become so familiar with the three evaluative criteria that they will truly *internalize* those criteria.

Gathering Pre-Instruction Data

To begin to collect evidence about her students' oral communication skills, during the first week of school, Cora randomly chooses six of her contemporary-issue speech topics for a pretest, a different set for each of her four classes. Then she randomly chooses six students in each class, assigns each student a speech topic, and gives those students an overnight period in which to prepare.

The following day, all students present their speeches to the class. After a short-course in camera technique provided by Cora's husband, one student in each class videotapes the speeches against a neutral chalkboard background that will provide no clues to indicate *when* the speeches were given.

Based on in-class observation of her students' oral "pretest" presentations (and informed by her three-criterion rubric), Cora concludes that this skill is one in which very few of her students possess substantial mastery. Although it's possible that her students received instruction in this skill in earlier grades, the "random sample" presentations in each of her four classes are remarkably weak. Cora realizes that she'll need to start with the basics, focusing on the skills and enabling subskills that her students will need to meet the evaluative criteria on her rubric and, ultimately, to develop into powerful, fluent public speakers. She opens her planning book, retrieves her list of skills and subskills, and gets to work.

Two Other Curricular Aims

In addition to the oral communication content standard, Cora also identifies several of her own curricular aims she wants to work on during the year—aims not necessarily embodied in any of the state-sanctioned content standards. One of those aims is for students to employ Standard American English (both orally and in writing) with few grammatical errors. As the school year progresses, Cora works on this objective whenever students supply any original writing and whenever they deliver oral reports or practice their extemporaneous speechmaking. During the school year, she tries to use her classroom tests as teaching tools related to this usage objective.

For example, one day Cora notices that several students in her third-period class and her sixth-period class are making the same kind of grammatical mistakes in their oral reports. They are violating subject-verb agreement, using plural verbs with singular sentences and vice versa. That evening, Cora whips up a short quiz on the topic.

When she sees the results of this quiz, Cora easily infers that most of her students need a serious dose of direct instruction about how subjects and verbs ought to agree with one another. In her weekly planning session, she incorporates that instruction into several upcoming lesson plans.

Cora also has a personal *affective* objective for the year, namely, that her students will gain confidence in their own oral communication skills. To promote that aim, she makes sure to praise her students' progress frequently and gives them numerous opportunities to discover how much their oral communication skills are improving. Next year, she intends to formally measure her students' growth in oral communication confidence, and she's already drafted a version of the self-report affective inventory she will administer to her students on an anonymous pretest/post-test basis.

Monitoring Progress and Modifying Approaches

Interestingly, at least to Cora, her students take a long time to master the oral communication skill. At the start of the school year, Cora had thought that if her students mastered the skill by the middle of the school year, she would devote little or no further instruction to it. Near mid-year, she has students in all her classes deliver a five-minute extemporaneous speech on a topic of their own choosing. When evaluated against the three-criterion rubric, these speeches indicate that more instruction is most definitely needed.

Because of her students' weak mid-year performances, Cora also decides to alter her instructional approach to some extent. She begins to devote much more attention to the use of peer critiquing, routinely charging a panel of three students with evaluating a classmate's oral presentation via the three-criterion rubric. These student panels describe their group-derived critiques to the presenter and, simultaneously, to the rest of the class. This peer-critiquing modification appears to make students more attentive to the rubric's three evaluative criteria. Cora is pleased with that particular consequence of her modified instructional tactics.

Post-Testing and Assembling Credible Evidence of Instructional Effectiveness

At the end of the school year, Cora assigns the remaining six contemporary issues speech topics to six *different* randomly selected students in each of her four classes. Once again, she gives the students an overnight preparation period, and once again, other students videotape their classmates' speeches against the same neutral background.

From all her classes combined, Cora winds up with 24 videotaped "post-tests" to contrast with the 24 videotaped "pretests" from the beginning of the school year. She calls on her husband to edit the four class sets of videotaped speeches (six pretests and six post-tests for each class) into a single videotape per class, with the pretest speeches and post-test speeches mixed together so that the edited sequencing will give viewers no idea which presentations were pretests and which were post-tests. Cora then gets a measure of her own instructional effectiveness regarding the "Appropriate Oral Communication" standard by asking four parents of students from her last year's classes to serve as judges of each of the four videotaped sets of speeches.

She provides the parent volunteers with the three-criterion rubric she used throughout the school year—the same criteria she relied on instructionally in each of her four classes. After the parents have made their judgments about the mixed-sequence video presentations, Cora identifies which speeches were pretests and which were post-tests. As it turns out, the post-test speeches received much higher blind-scored marks from the parent-judges than did the pretest speeches. This was true in all four classes, where parent-judges' scores indicated that at least five of the six blind-scored best student presentations were always post-test presentations. In one class, all six of the best parent-judged presentations had been delivered at post-test time.

Based on this evidence, Cora concludes that the instruction she devoted to students' mastery of this significant grade-level benchmark was effective. She is, of course, delighted with that result.

Although the results of the parents' year-end, blind-scored judgments provide Cora with definitive, nonpartisan, and highly credible evidence, she's been using her three-criterion rubric to gauge her instructional effectiveness throughout the school year. She's been routinely evaluating oral presentations with the rubric, then providing some form of individualized feedback. She's been monitoring an ever-growing file of rubric-based, peer-completed critiques. In other words, although Cora chooses to carry out a fairly elaborate pretest/post-test comparison in order to appraise her instructional success, she also engages in a set of ongoing, less formal assessment-based activities that allow her to monitor the quality of her teaching and make sure that it remains strong.

Test Better, Teach Better

Cora relied heavily on assessments as she made the many instructional decisions she was called on to make throughout the year. She used the sample test items to help clarify the state's curricular aims. She used her own pretests to confirm her intuition about her students' weak oral communication skills. She discovered from mid-year assessments that she needed to continue to supply instruction related to this skill because her students had not yet mastered it. She employed an inventive blind-scored comparison of her students' videotaped pretest and post-test oral presentations to secure hard evidence that her instruction related to this important skill was genuinely effective. Cora also relied on short, special-purpose tests (such as the short quiz dealing with subject-verb agreement) to guide her when she spotted potential student deficits. And, happily, she will be moving next year into the formal, anonymous assessment of her students' affect.

Clearly, there is more to teaching than just testing. But if you, as a teacher, recognize and take advantage of the dividends that derive from instructionally focused testing, then your instruction will almost always get better . . . and your students will almost always learn more. Cora's fictitious tale indicates several ways that testing can help teaching. It almost always will.

Index

About the Author

W. JAMES POPHAM IS PROFESSOR EMERITUS, UCLA GRADUATE SCHOOL OF Education and Information Studies. He has spent most of his career as a teacher, largely at UCLA, where for three decades he taught courses in instructional methods for prospective teachers and courses in evaluation and measurement for master's and doctoral degree candidates. In 1997, Dr. Popham received a Lifetime Achievement Award in Educational Research and Measurement from the California Educational Research Association. In January 2000, he was recognized by *UCLA Today* as one of the university's top 20 professors of the 20th century.

In 1968, Dr. Popham established IOX Assessment Associates, a research and development group that has created statewide student achievement tests for a dozen states. He is the author of 25 books and nearly 200 journal articles, a former president of the American Educational Research Association (AERA), and the founding editor of AERA's quarterly journal, *Educational Evaluation and Policy Analysis*.

● ● ● ● ●

Related ASCD Resources: Assessment—
Large-Scale and in the Classroom

Audiotapes

Classroom Assessment for Student Learning by Ken O'Connor (#203098)
Improving Student Performance Through Testing and Standards by
  Ronald Costello (#200138)
Promoting Parents' and Policymakers' Assessment Literacy by W. James Popham
  (#200106)
A Systematic Approach to Rubric Development by Ruth Loring (#297110)

Multimedia

Assessing Student Performance: An ASCD Professional Inquiry Kit by
  Judith A. Arther (#196214)
Promoting Learning Through Student Data: An ASCD Professional Inquiry Kit
  by Marian Leibowitz (#999004)

Online Professional Development

Go to ASCD's Home page (http://www.ascd.org) and click on Professional
  Development. ASCD Professional Development Online Courses in
  Assessment include "Designing Performance Assessments," "Student
  Portfolios: Getting Started in Your Classroom," and "Teacher Behaviors
  That Promote Assessment for Learning."

Print Products

Educational Leadership (February 2003): Using Data to Improve Student Achieve-
  ment (#103031)
An Introduction to Using Portfolios in the Classroom by Charlotte Danielson
  and Leslye Arbrutyn (#197171)
Great Performances: Creating Classroom-Based Assessment Tasks by Larry Lewin
  and Betty Jean Shoemaker (#198184)
The Truth About Testing: An Educator's Call to Action by W. James Popham
  (#101030)

Videotapes

How to Prepare Students for Standardized Tests (#401014)
Redesigning Assessment (3-tape series with 3 facilitator's guides) (#614237)
Using Classroom Assessment to Guide Instruction (3-tape series with facilita-*
  tor's guide) (#402286)
Using Standards, Tape 2: Improving Curriculum and Assessment (#400264)

For additional resources, visit us on the World Wide Web (http://www.ascd.
org), send an e-mail message to member@ascd.org, call the ASCD Service
Center (1-800-933-ASCD or 703-578-9600, then press 2), send a fax to 703-
575-5400, or write to Information Services, ASCD, 1703 N. Beauregard St.,
Alexandria, VA 22311-1714 USA.